SUGAR SKULLS
Coloring Book for Adults

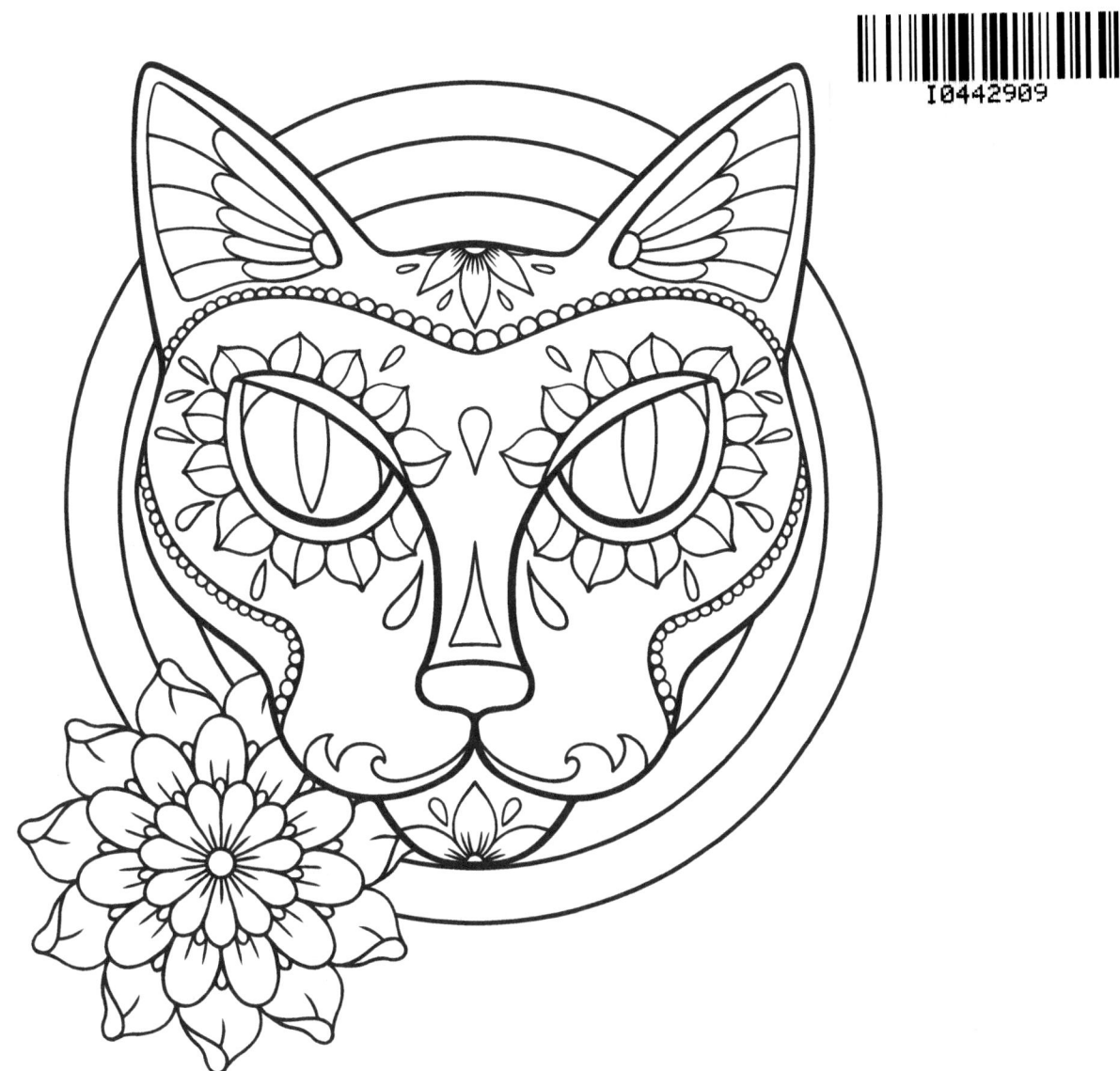

Vanessa Bentley

Copyright © Vanessa Bentley 2020

All rights reserved. No part of this publication may be reproduced, distributed, or transmitted in any form or by any means, including photocopying, recording, or other electronic or mechanical methods, without the prior written, dated and signed permission of the copyright owner.

40 original Illustrations of Sugar Skulls, Sugar Skull Women and Cats for you to color. Some are really easy and some are complex enough to keep your mind off all your worries for a few hours.

A variety of materials can be used to color these images, from color pencils to markers. To prevent bleed-through when coloring, place a blank sheet of paper or card stock between the pages.

Images have been printed on one side of the page only.

All images in this book are original drawings and designs by Vanessa Bentley.

www.vanessabentley.com

The Benefits of Coloring

Not everyone can draw or paint, that is where coloring books are great. The artist creates the image and puts it out there for someone else to complete the work by adding color in the medium of their choice. Many coloring book artists are pleasantly surprised when they get to see how colorists bring their images to life. So the artist and colorist are now in fact collaborators in the project.

Participating in a creativity such as coloring in occupies the part of the brain that deals with stress and worry. How? Well, when you color in you have to decide what you are going to color, what medium to use, what color or color combinations you are going to use and how you are going to color it.

Many retirement homes have started giving coloring pages to their residents to color in. It is not only good for hand eye coordination, but it is uplifting, relaxing and gives people a sense of accomplishment.

How to Color in

I believe that you should go with what you feel. Practice makes perfect and as you color more and more, you will get to know which colors you like putting together. If you are worried that you will mess up your image, you may make a copy of the page and practice on that copy.

If you want to learn more about coloring techniques, there are many tutorials on YouTube that will help you advance as a colorist.

Happy coloring!

Thank you for purchasing this book. I hope that you found the illustrations fun and interesting to color in.

If you enjoyed the book then I would be incredibly grateful if you would share your experience by either rating or leaving a few words in the review section where you purchased this book online.

Your feedback is important and helps me to continue creating work like this.

Vanessa Bentley

Also by Vanessa Bentley

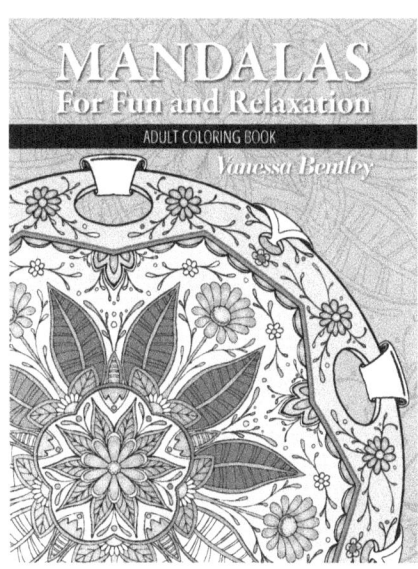 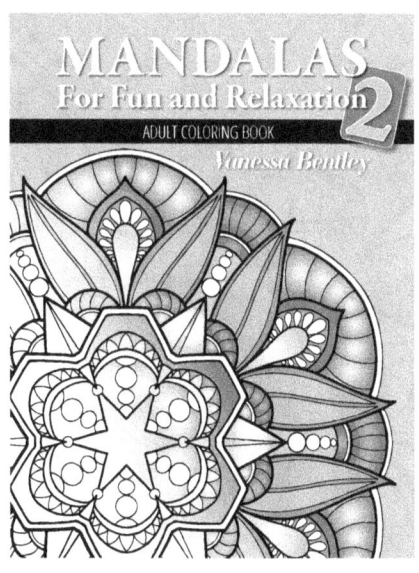

MANDALAS
For Fun and Relaxation

MANDALAS
For Fun and Relaxation 2

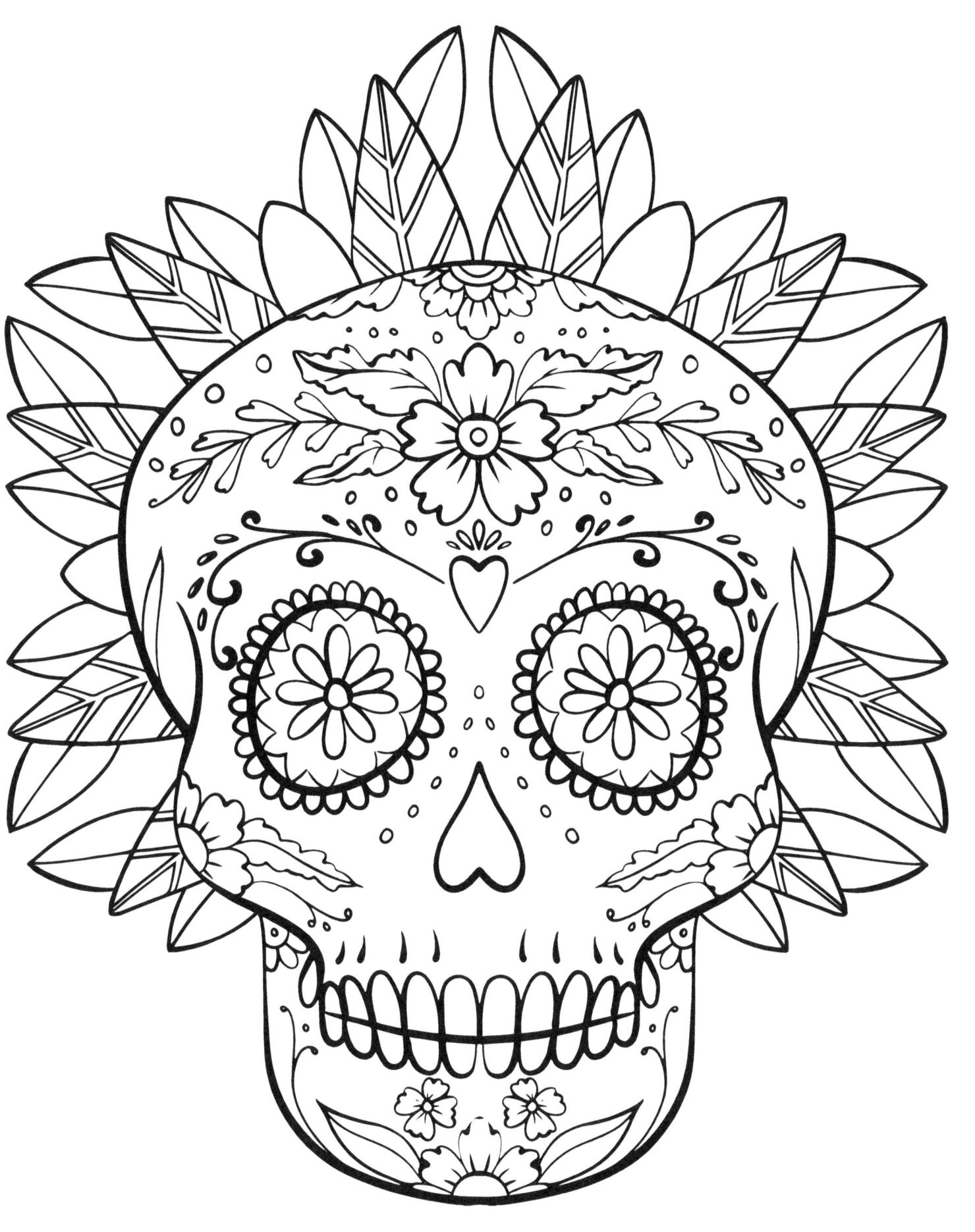

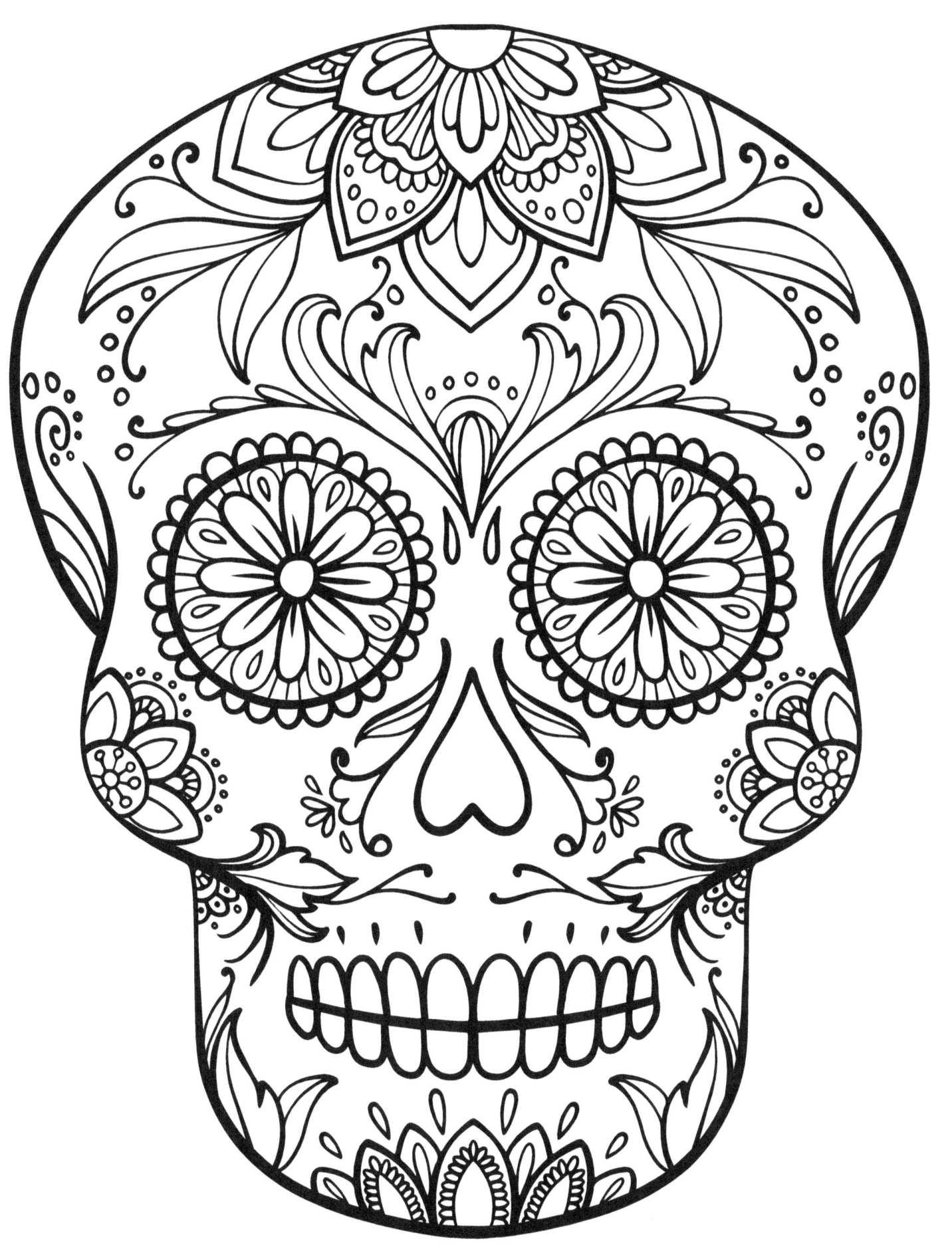

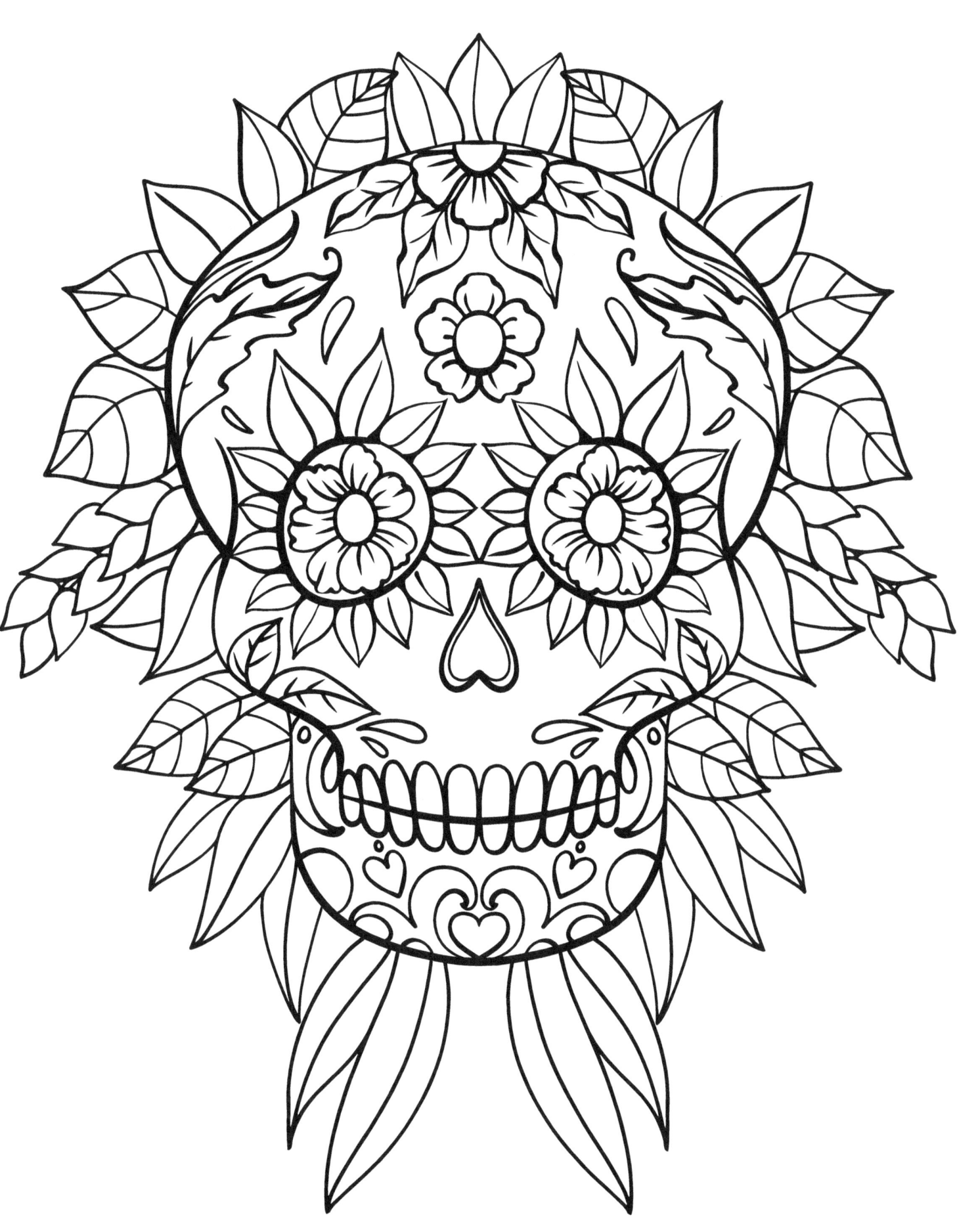

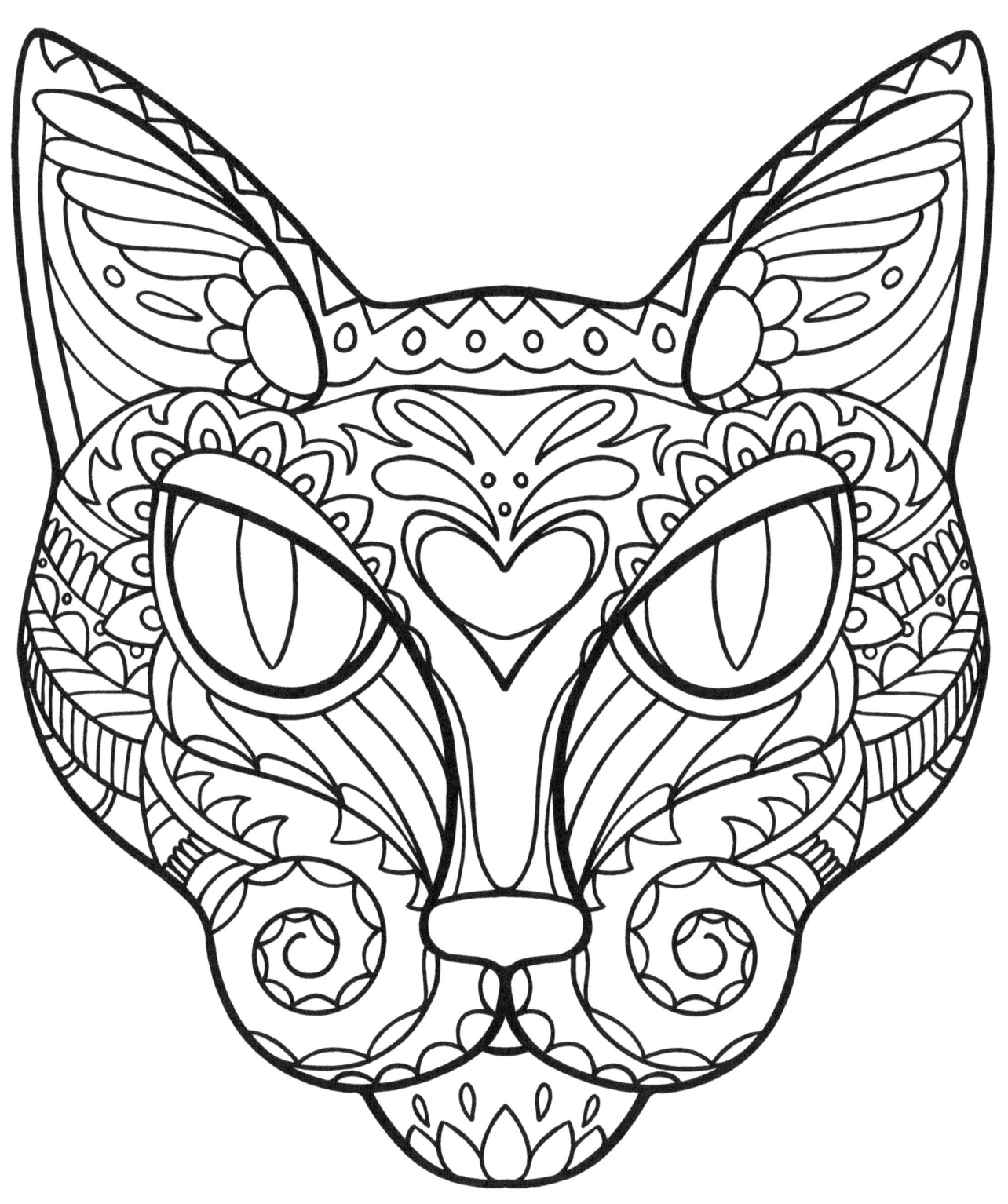

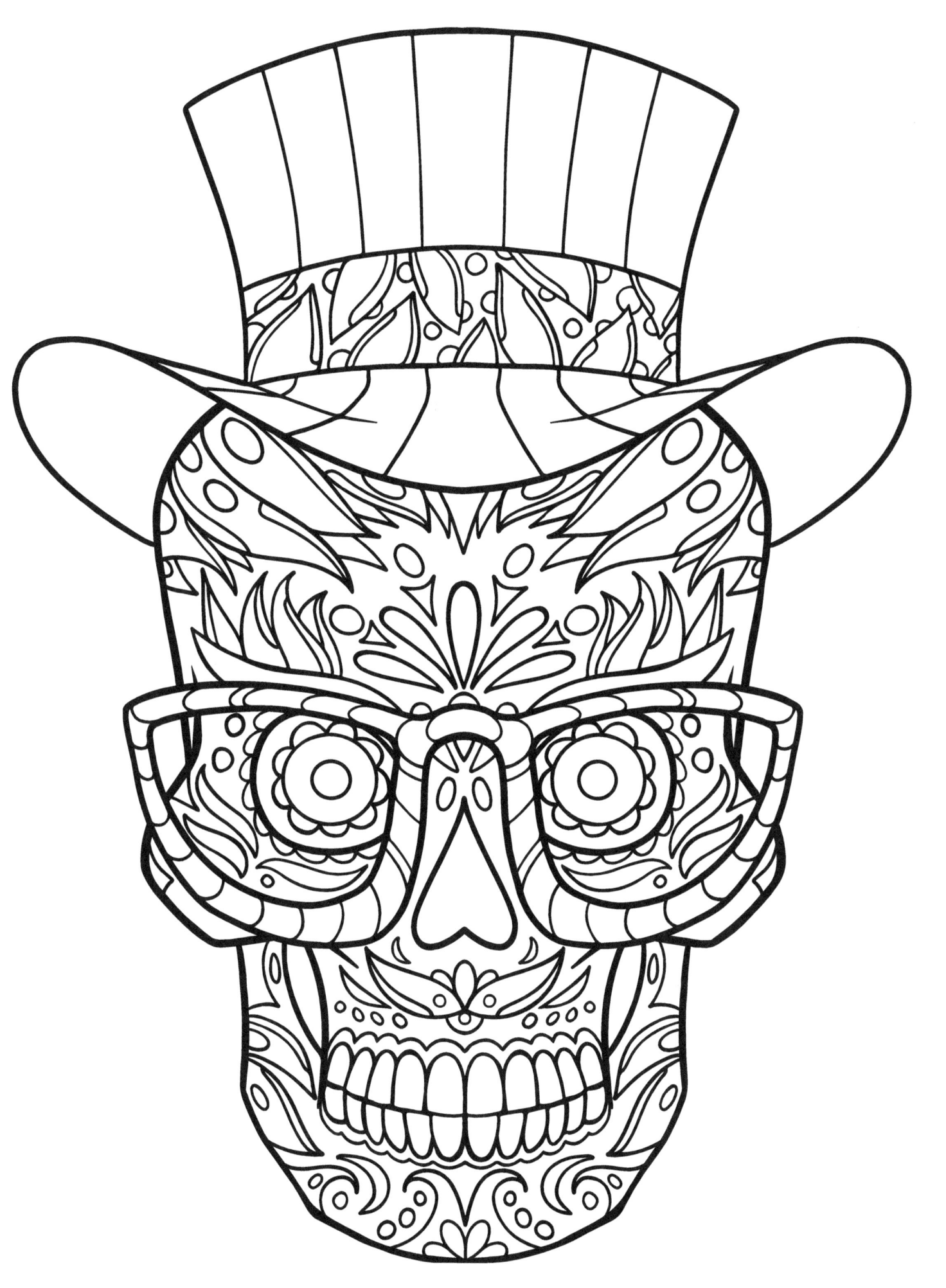

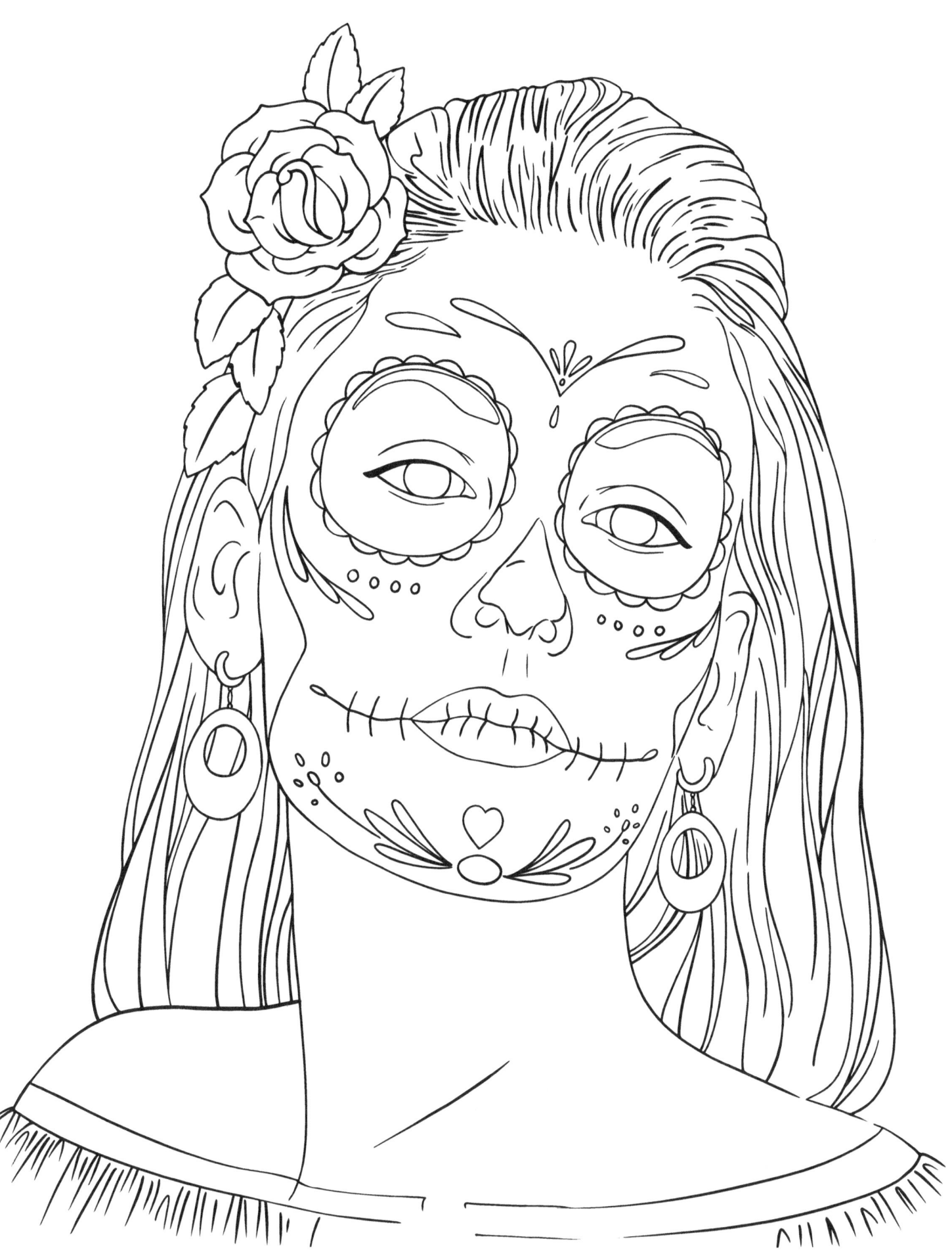

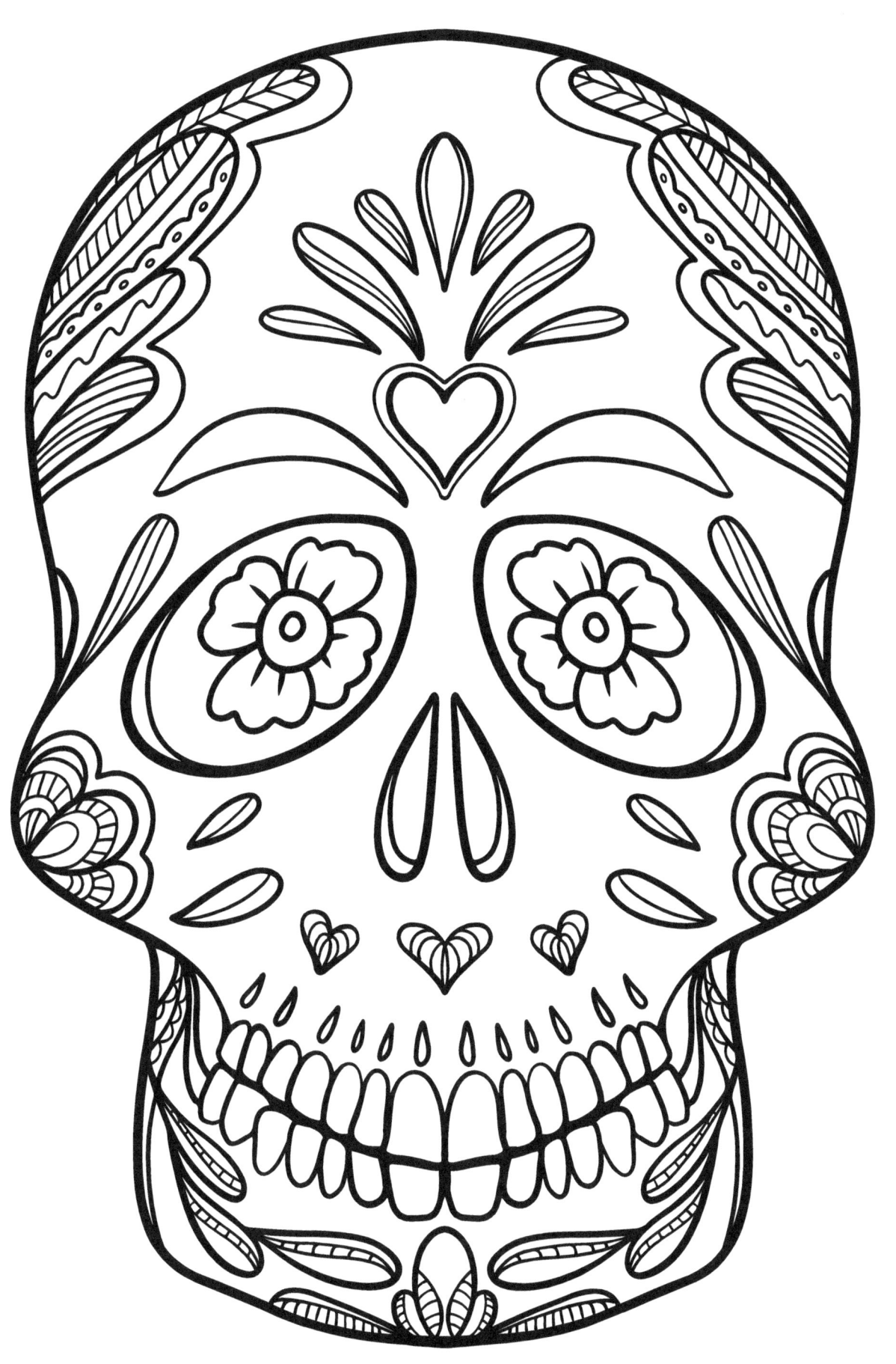

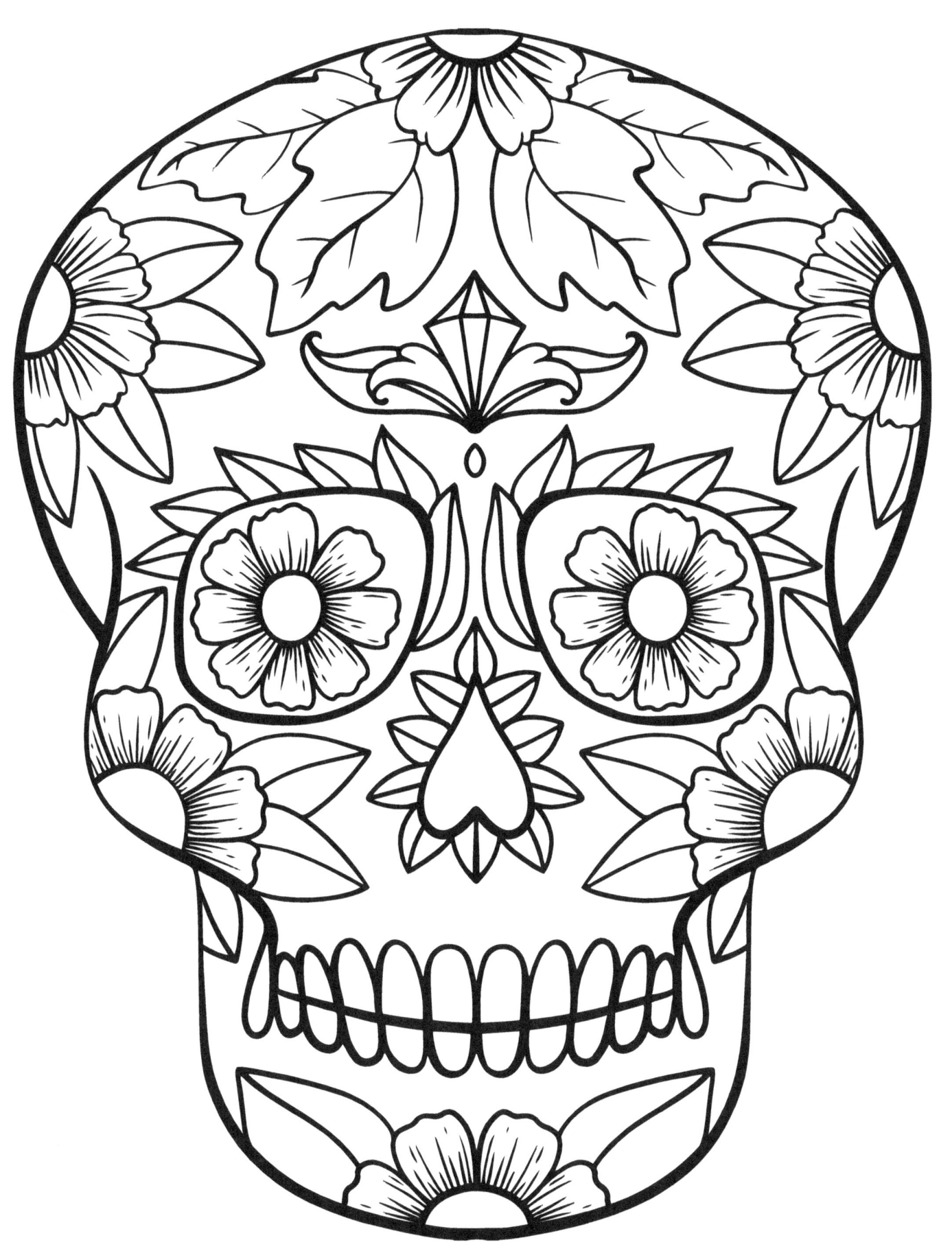

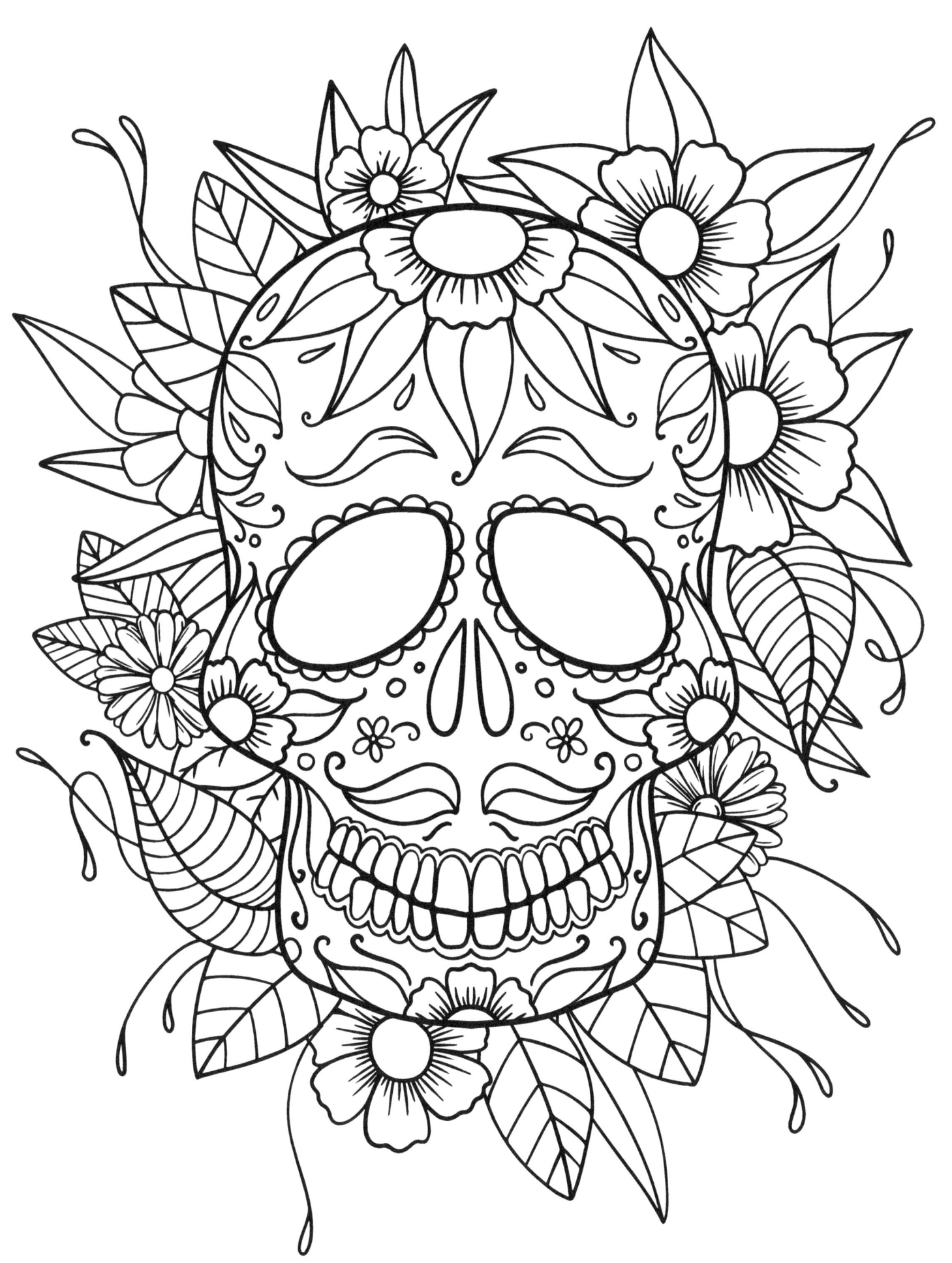

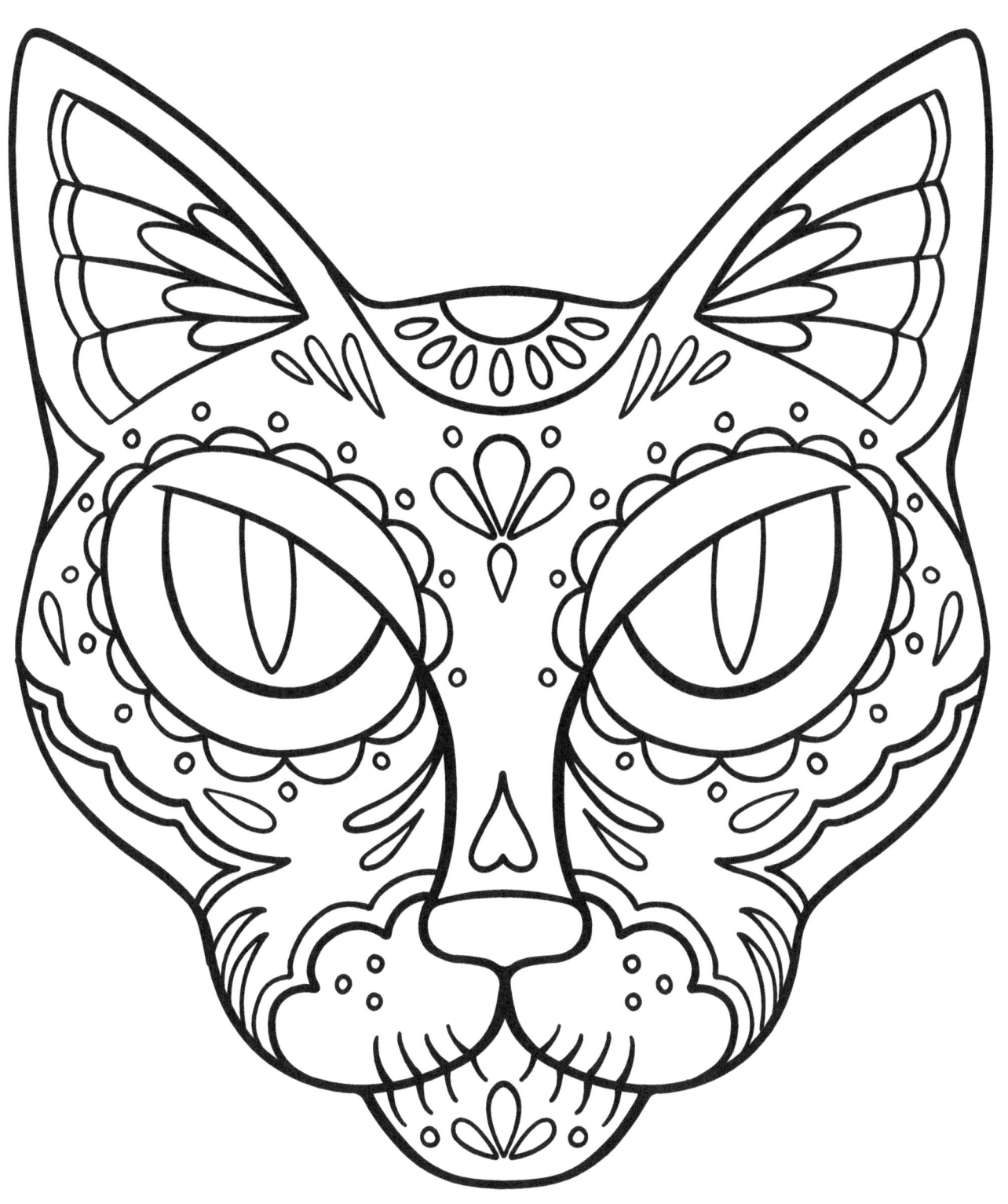

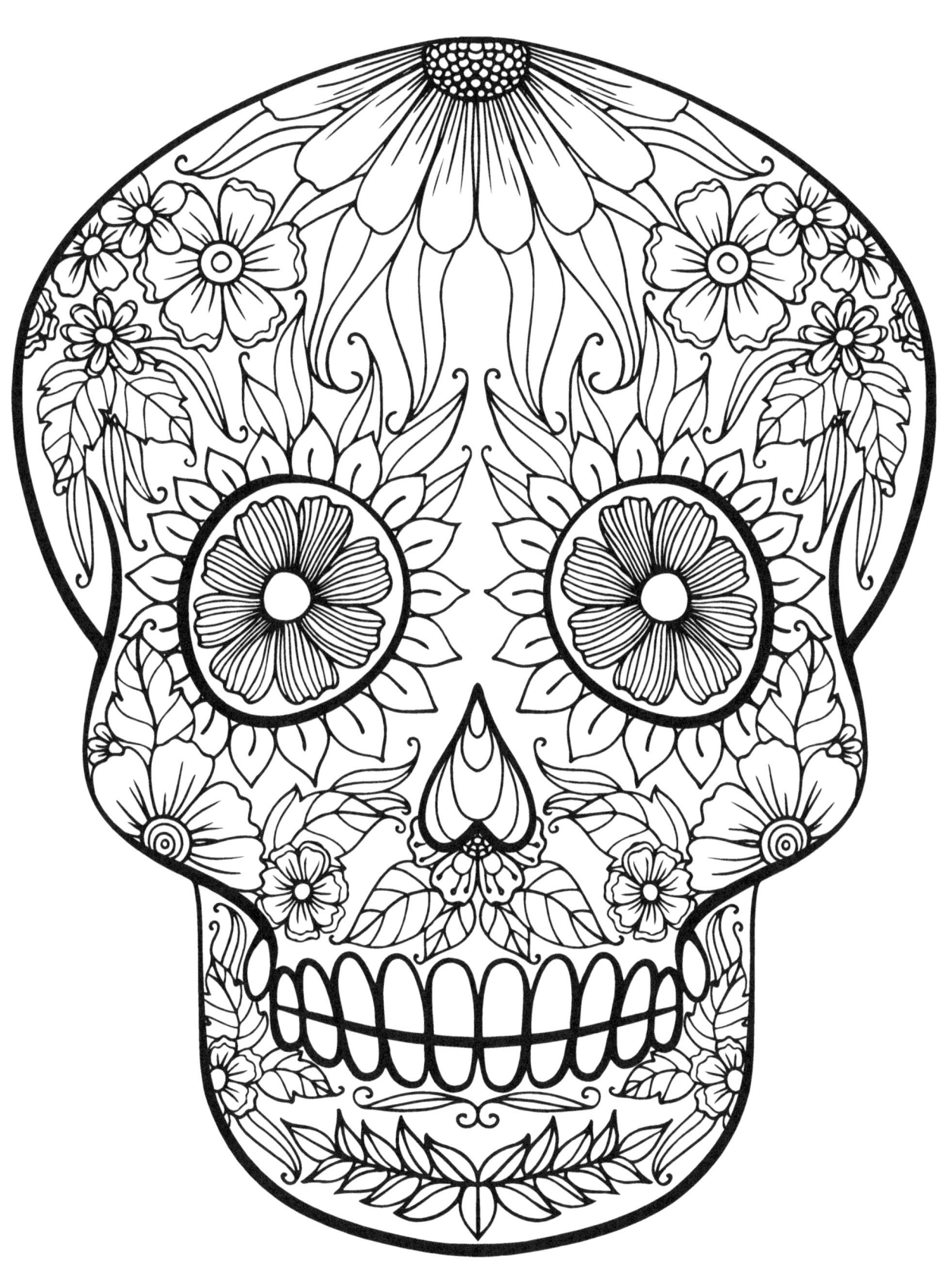

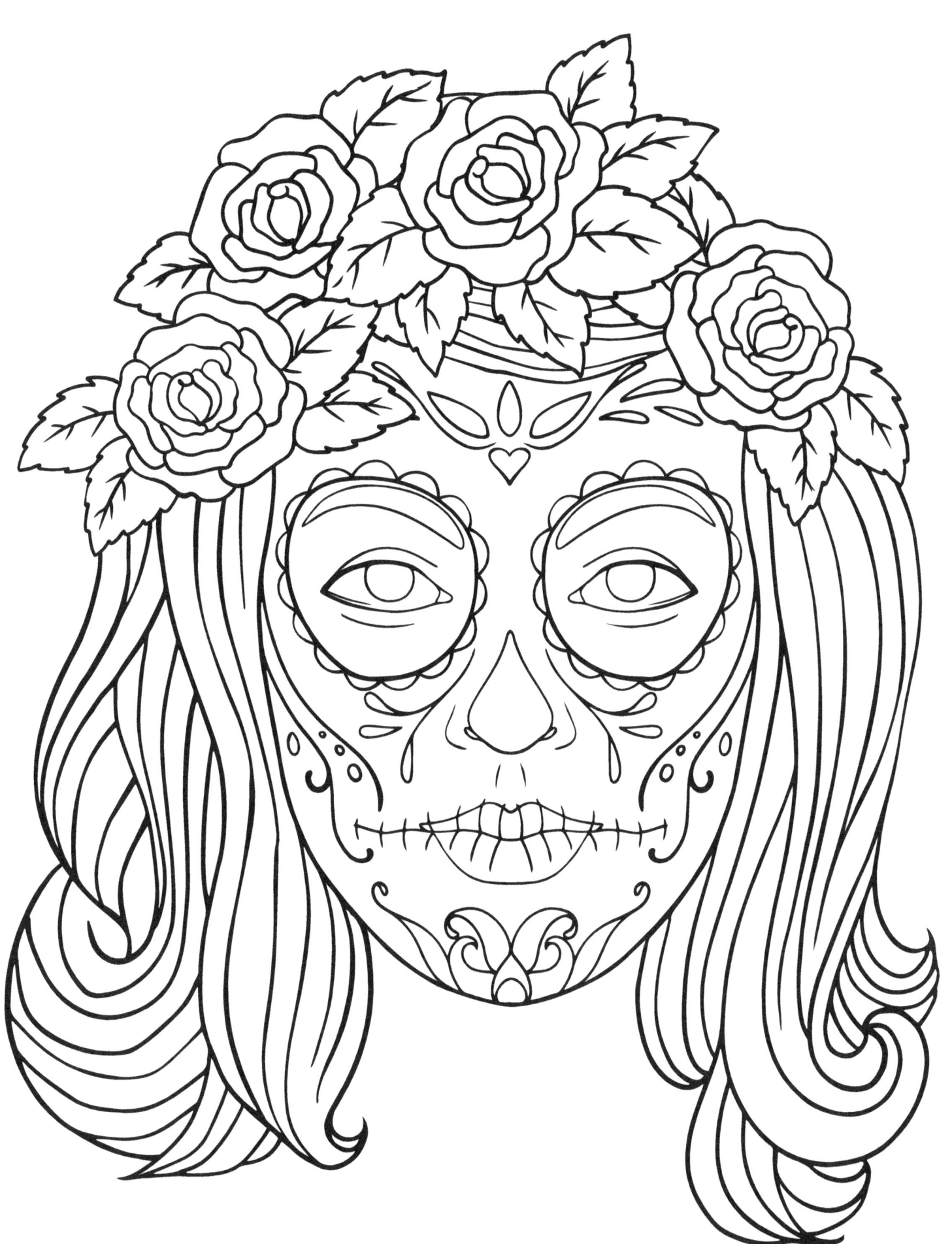

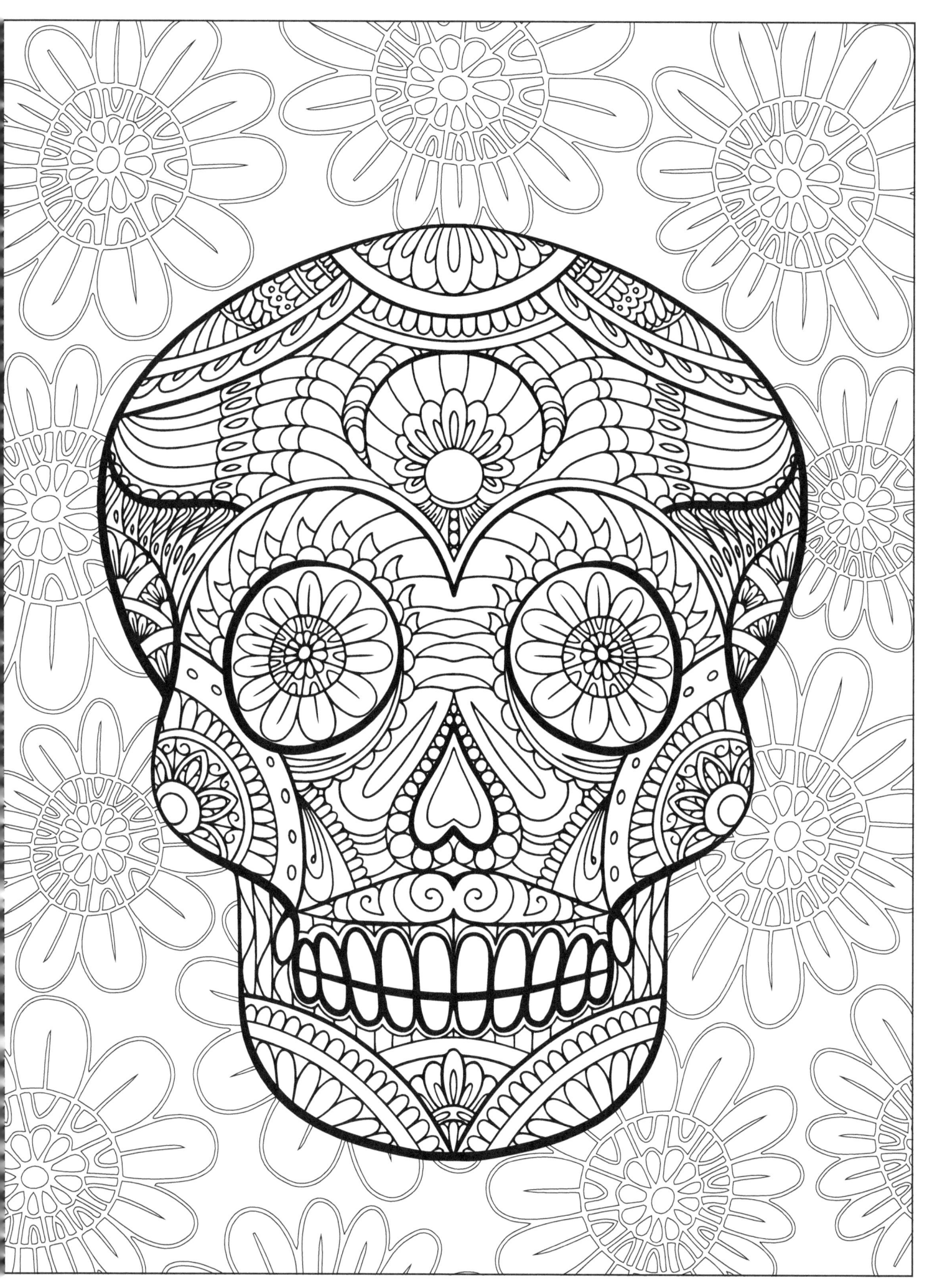

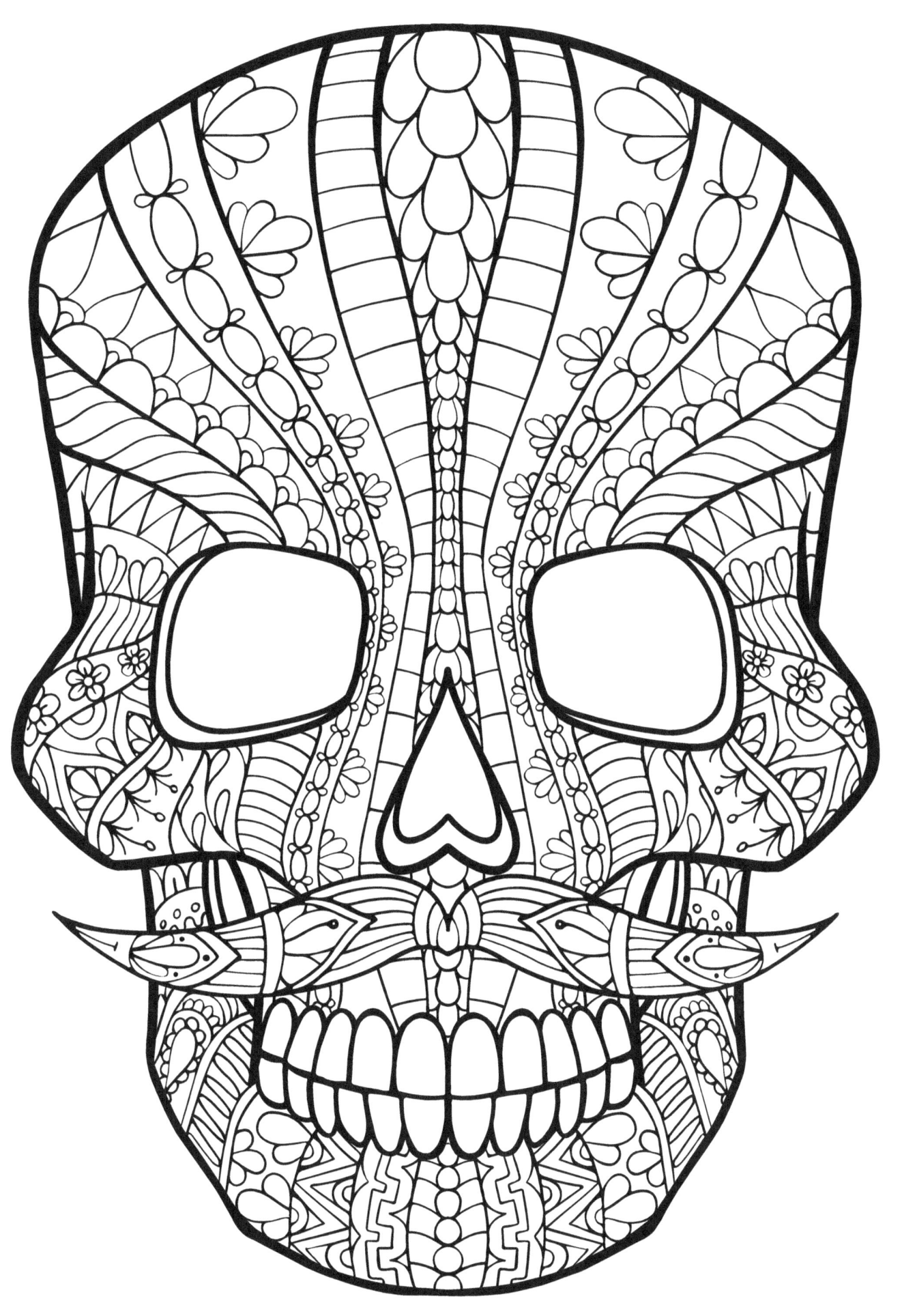

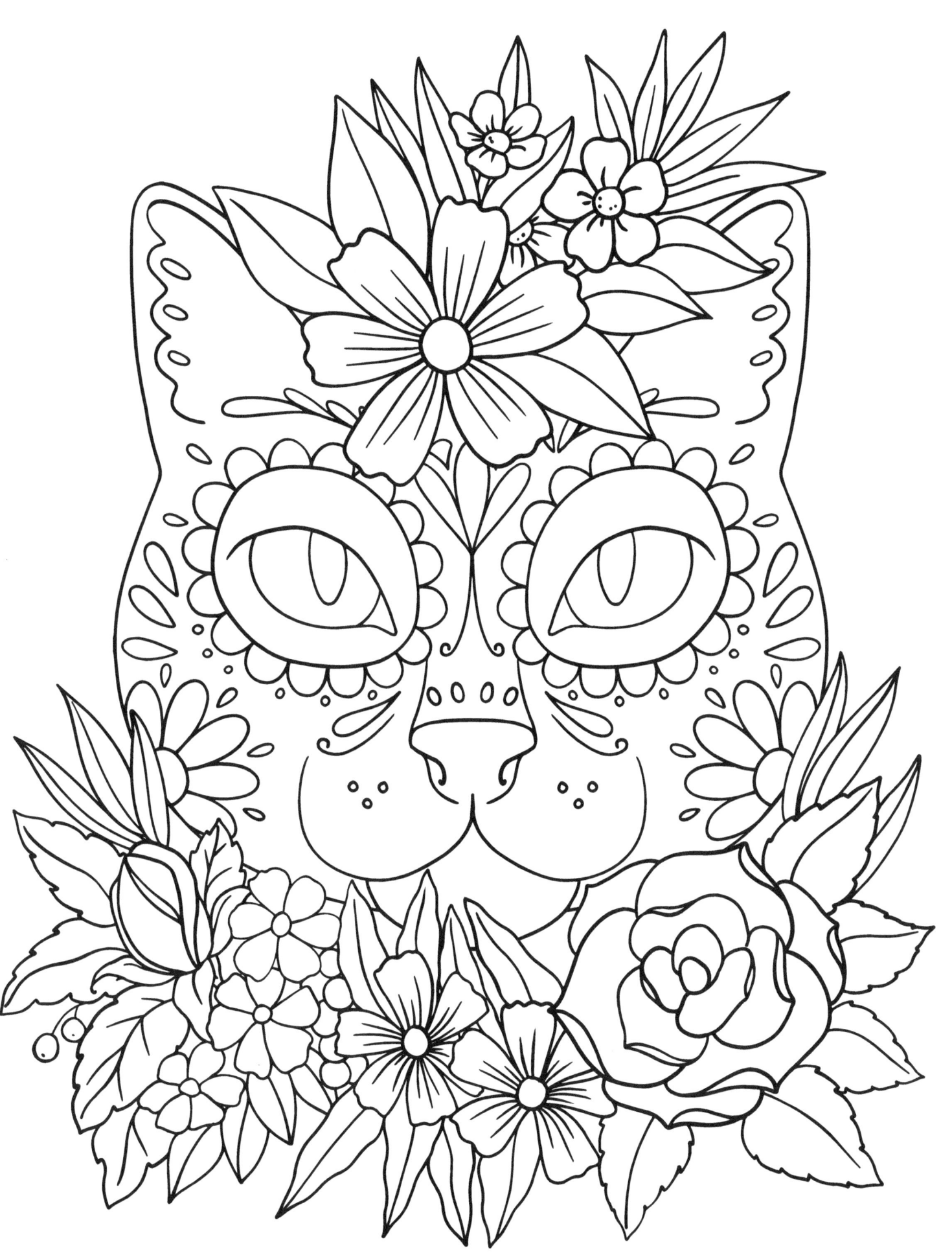

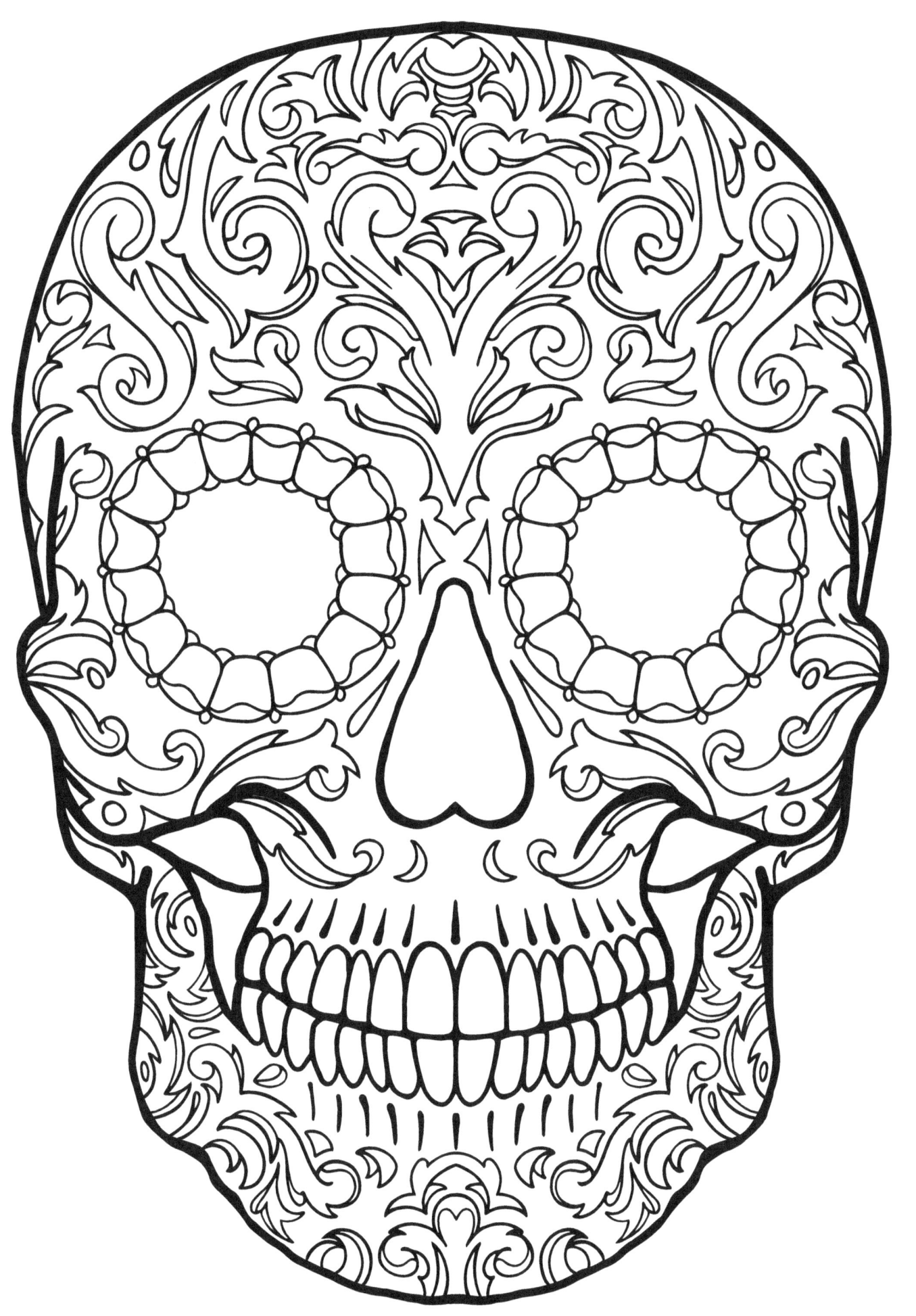

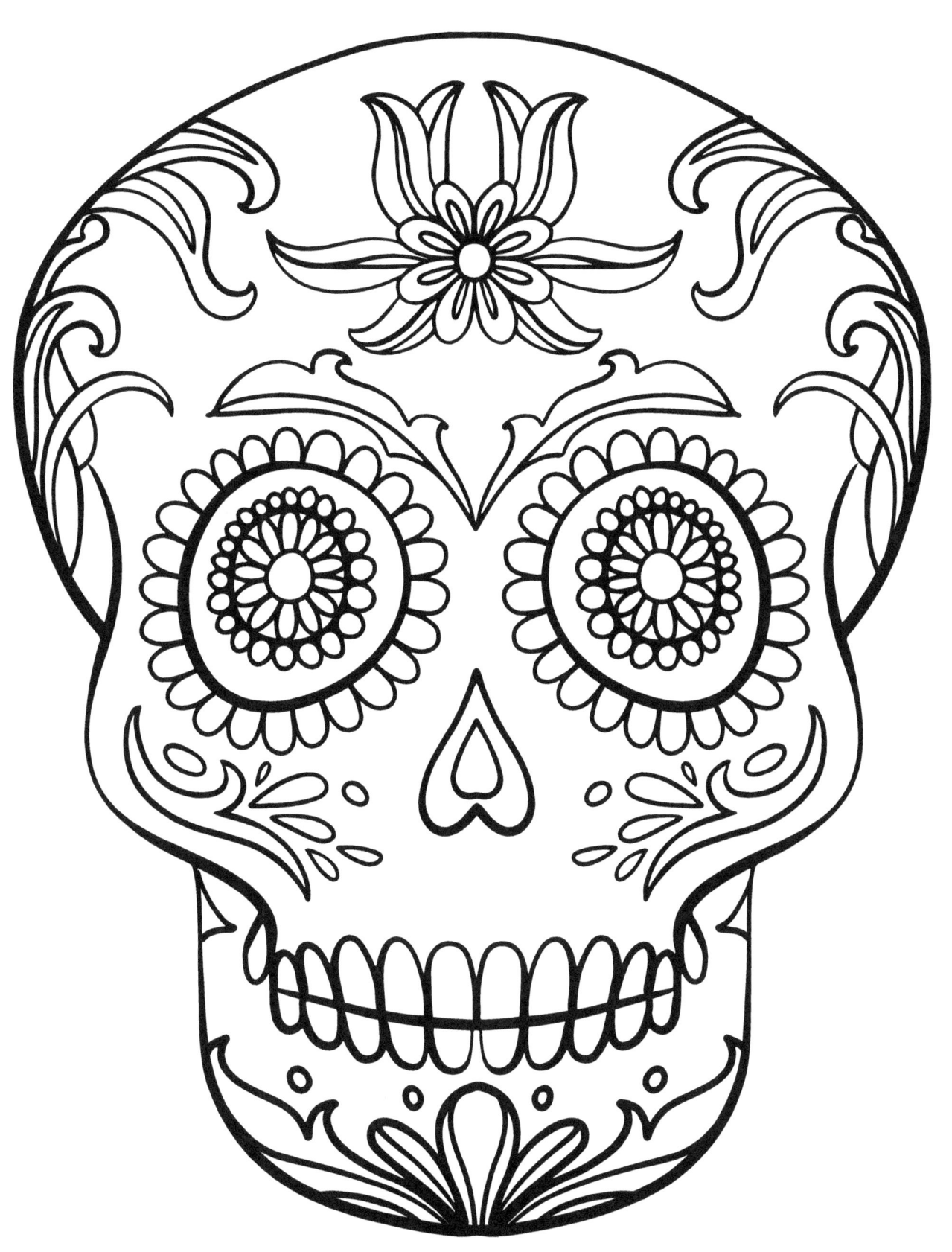

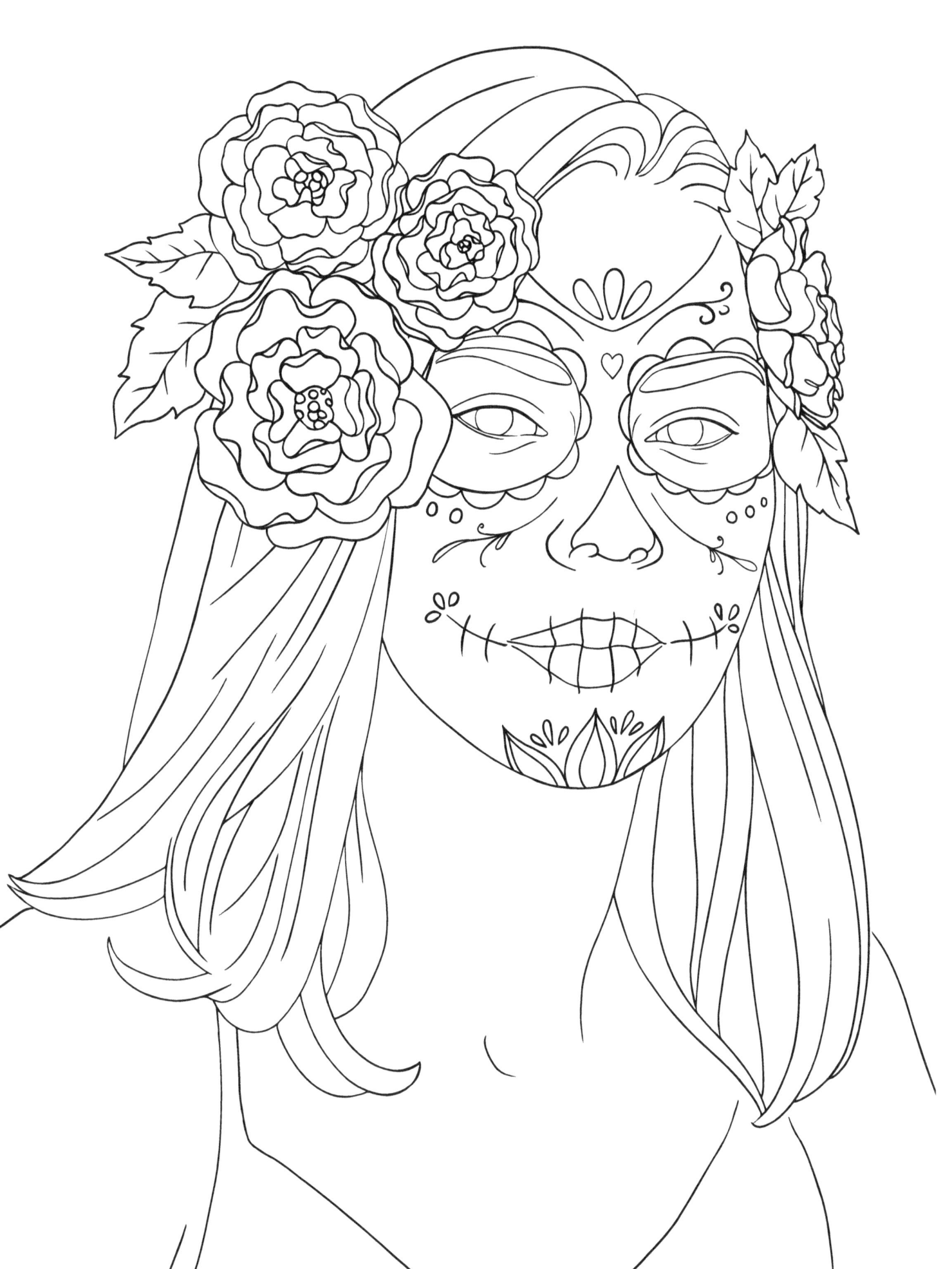

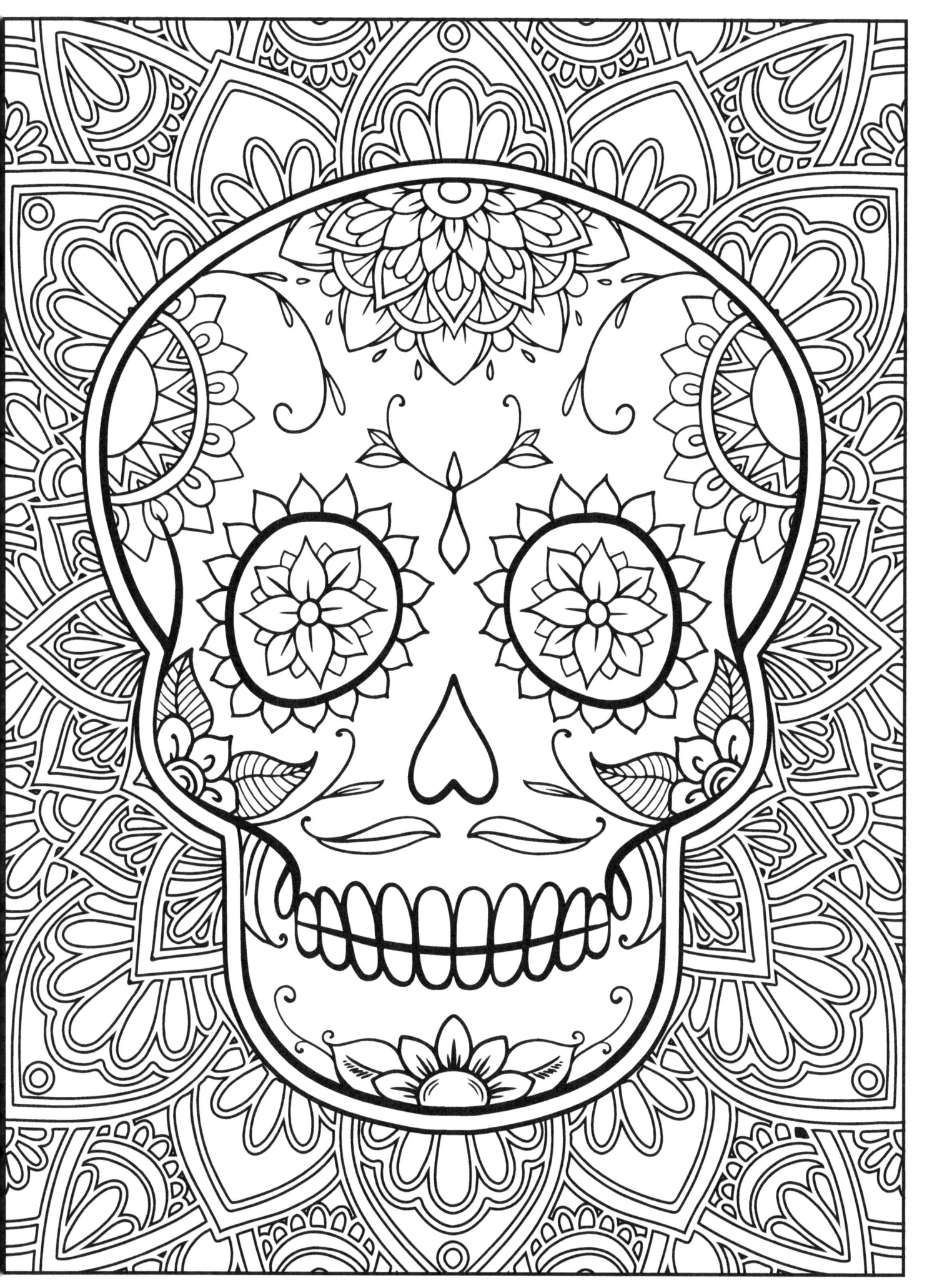

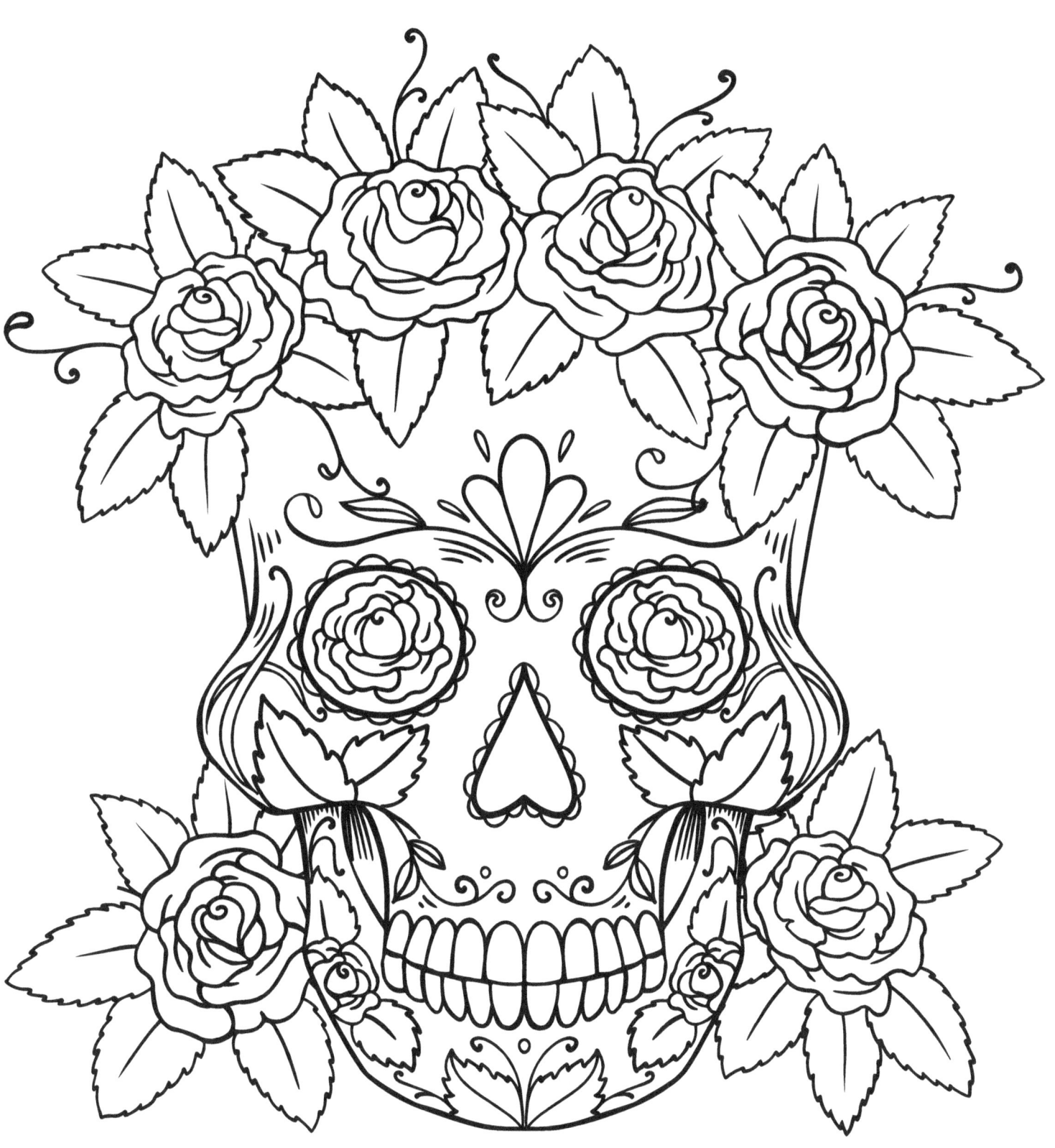

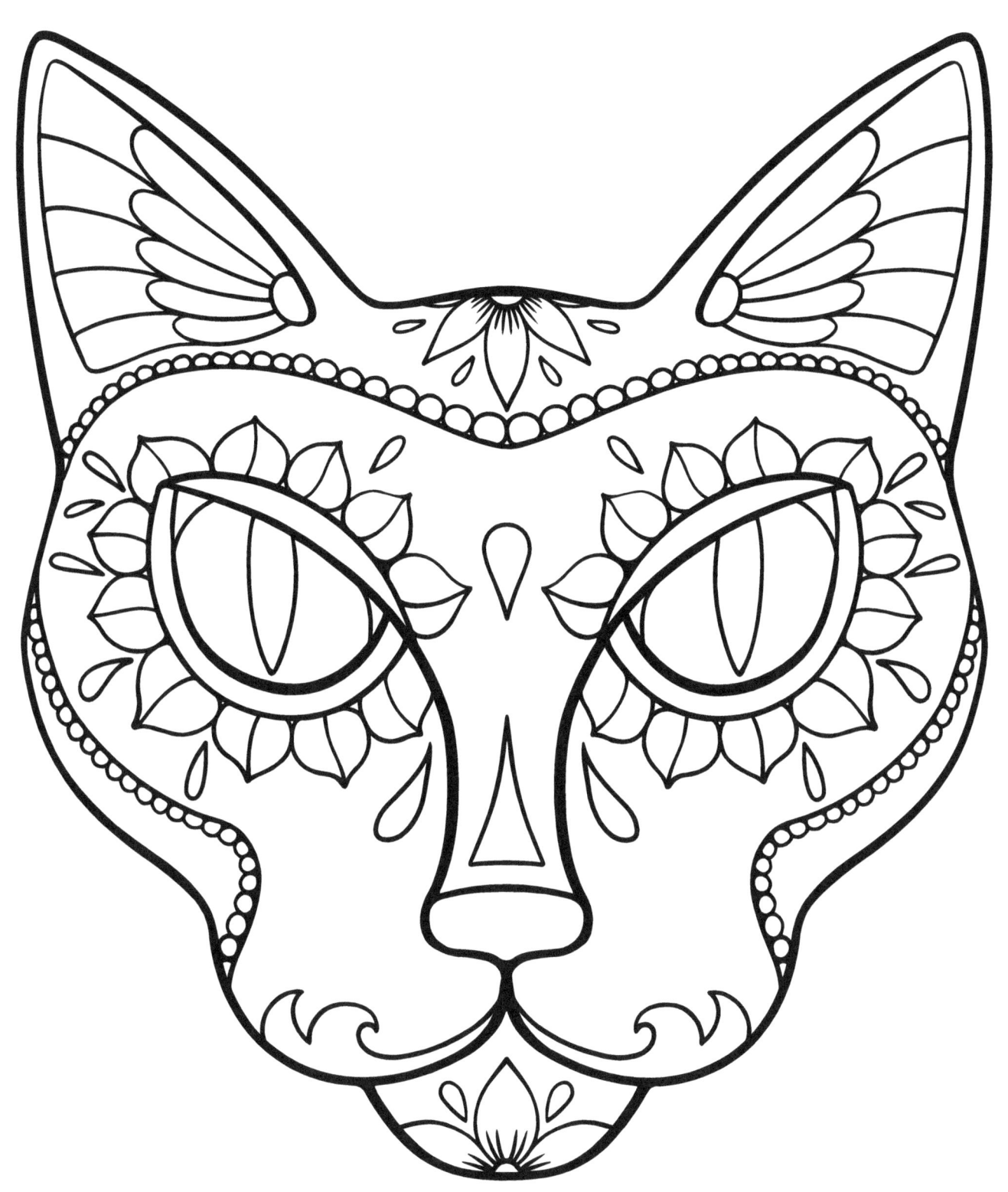

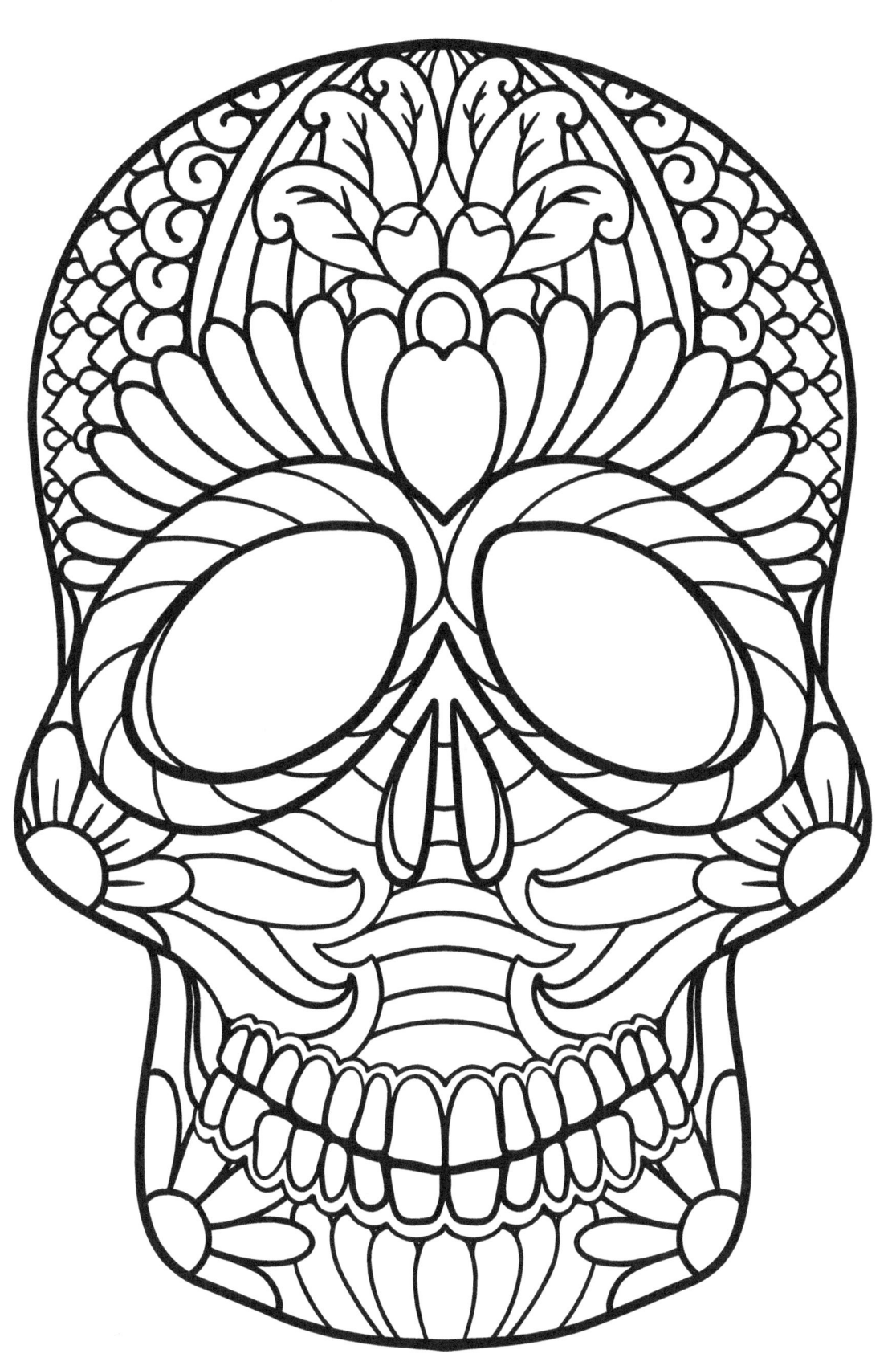

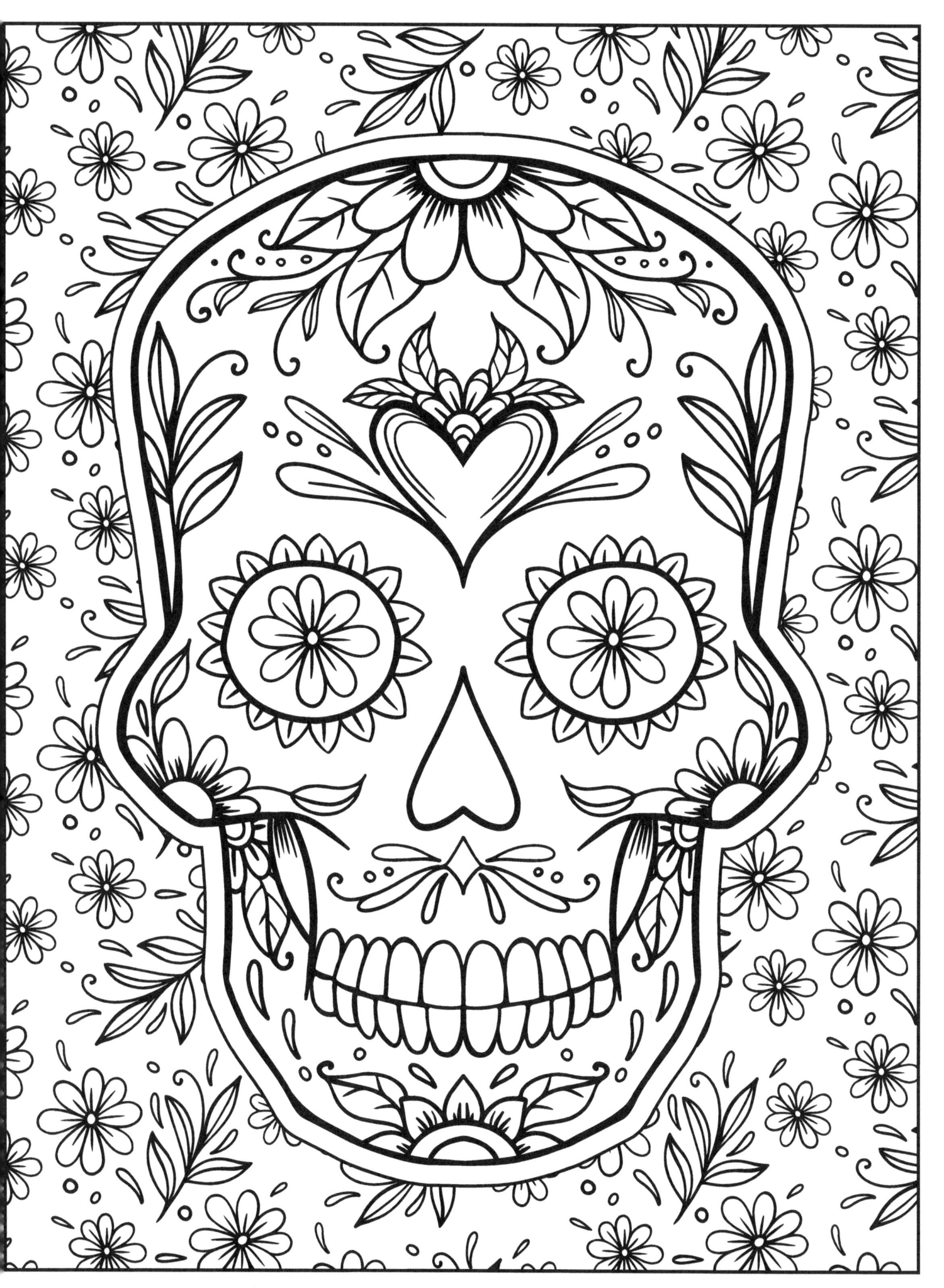

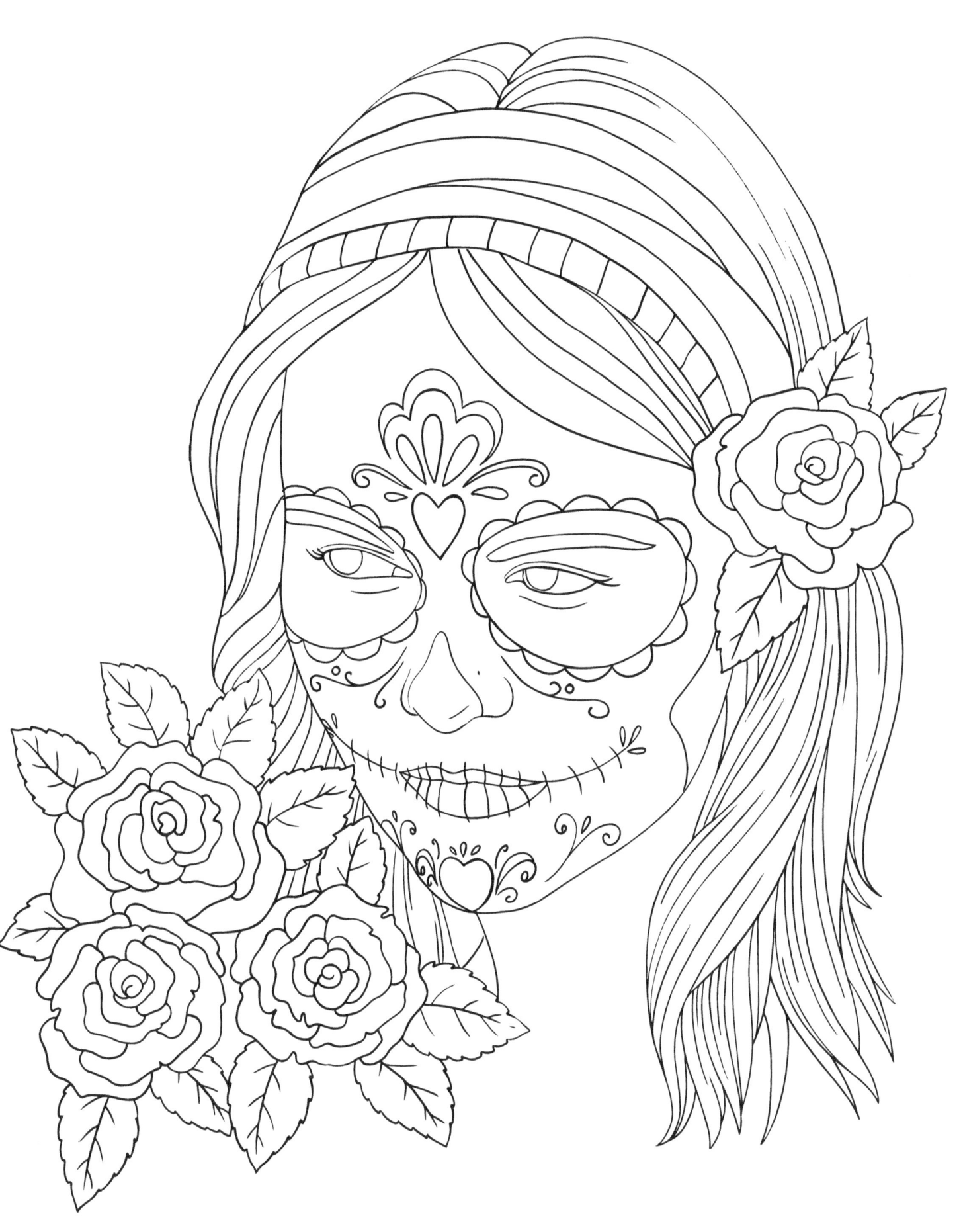

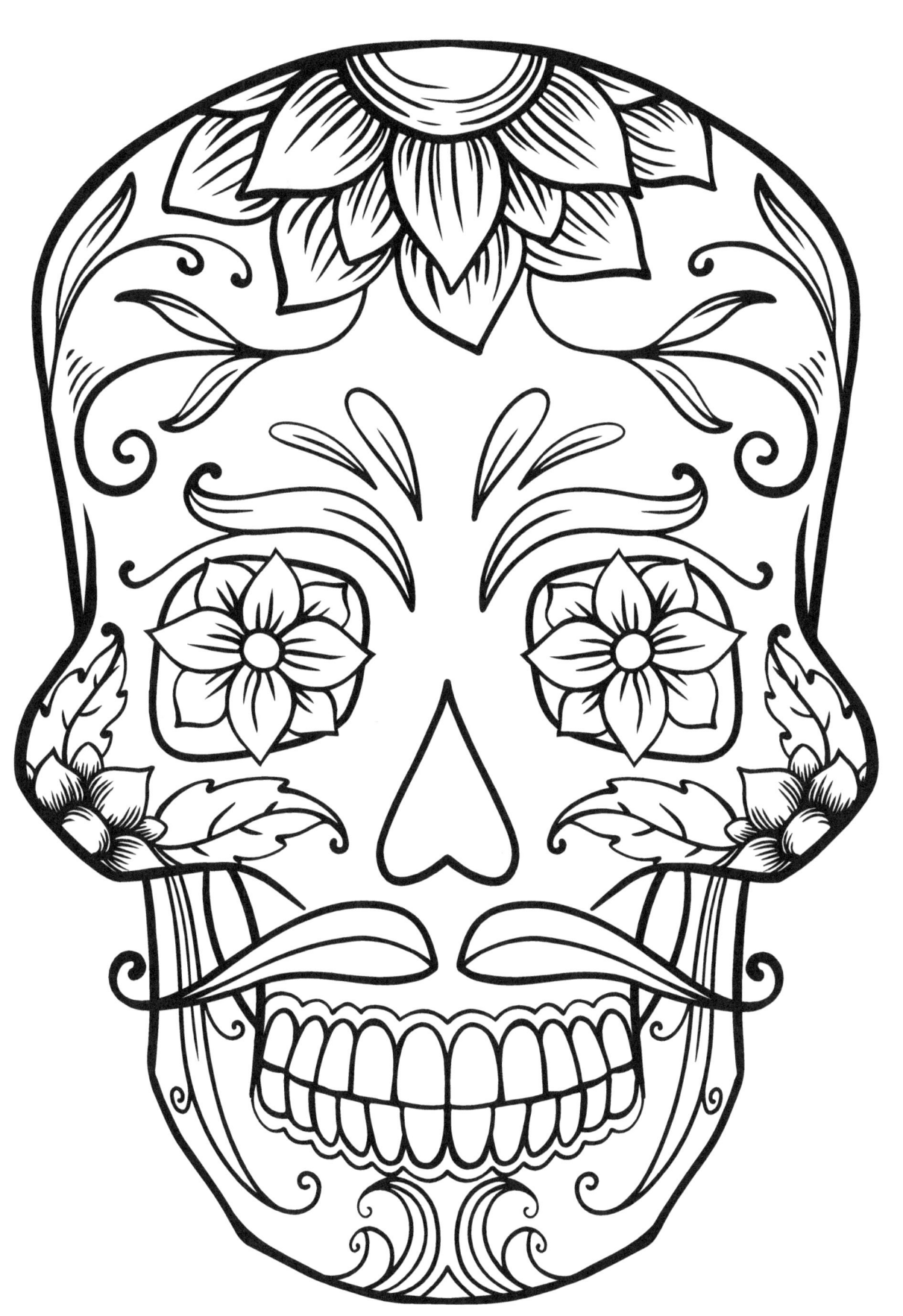

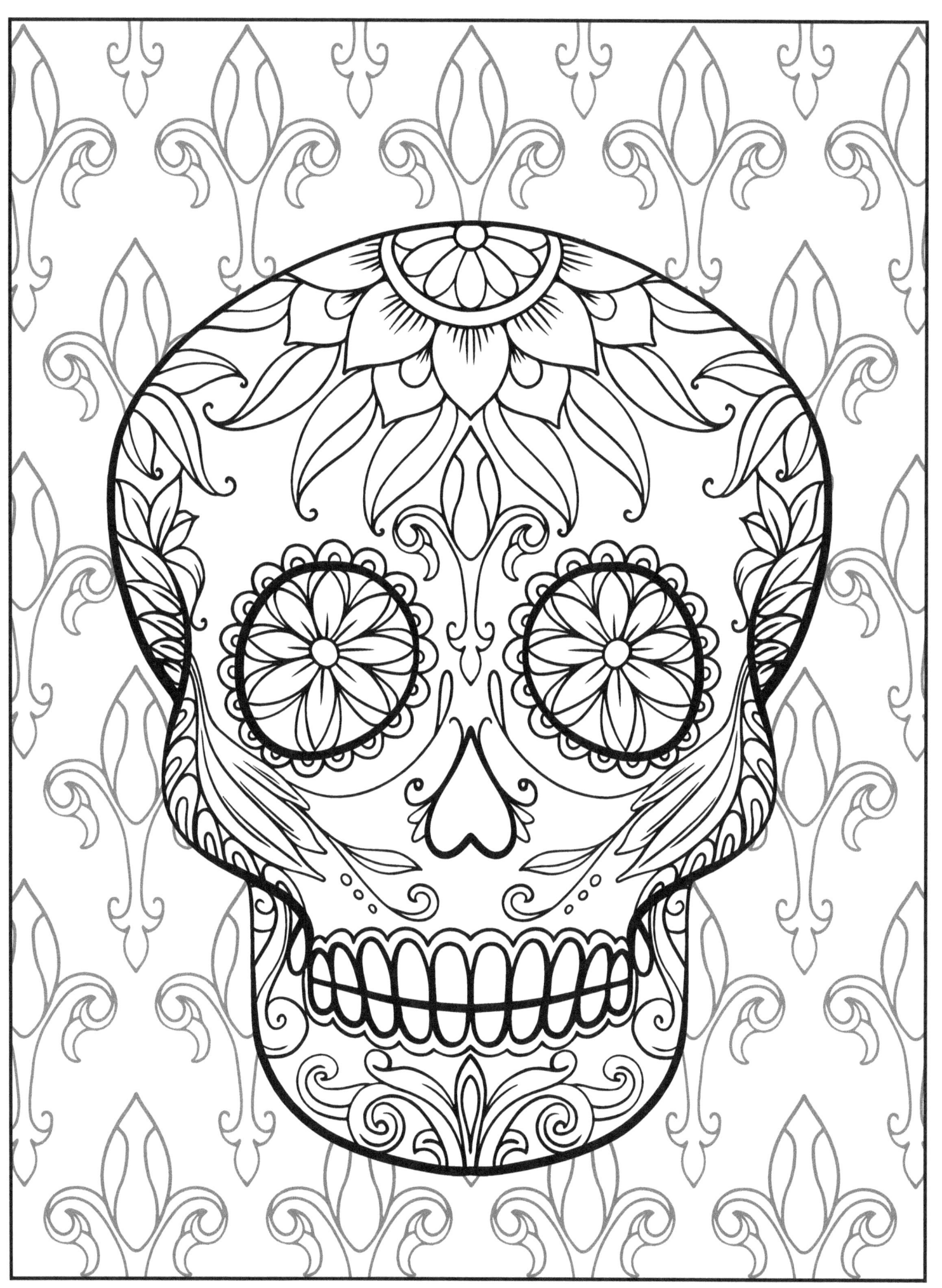

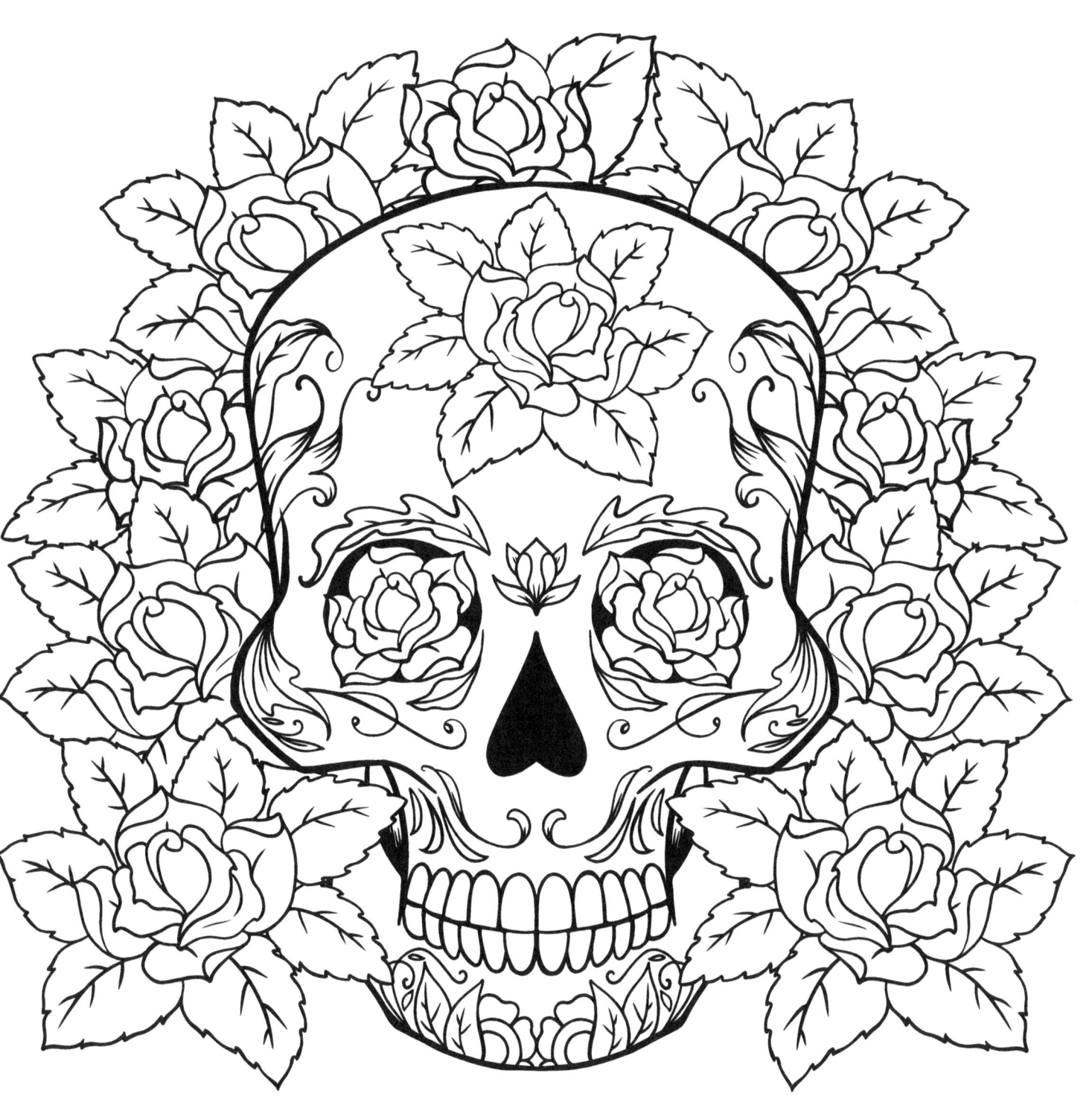

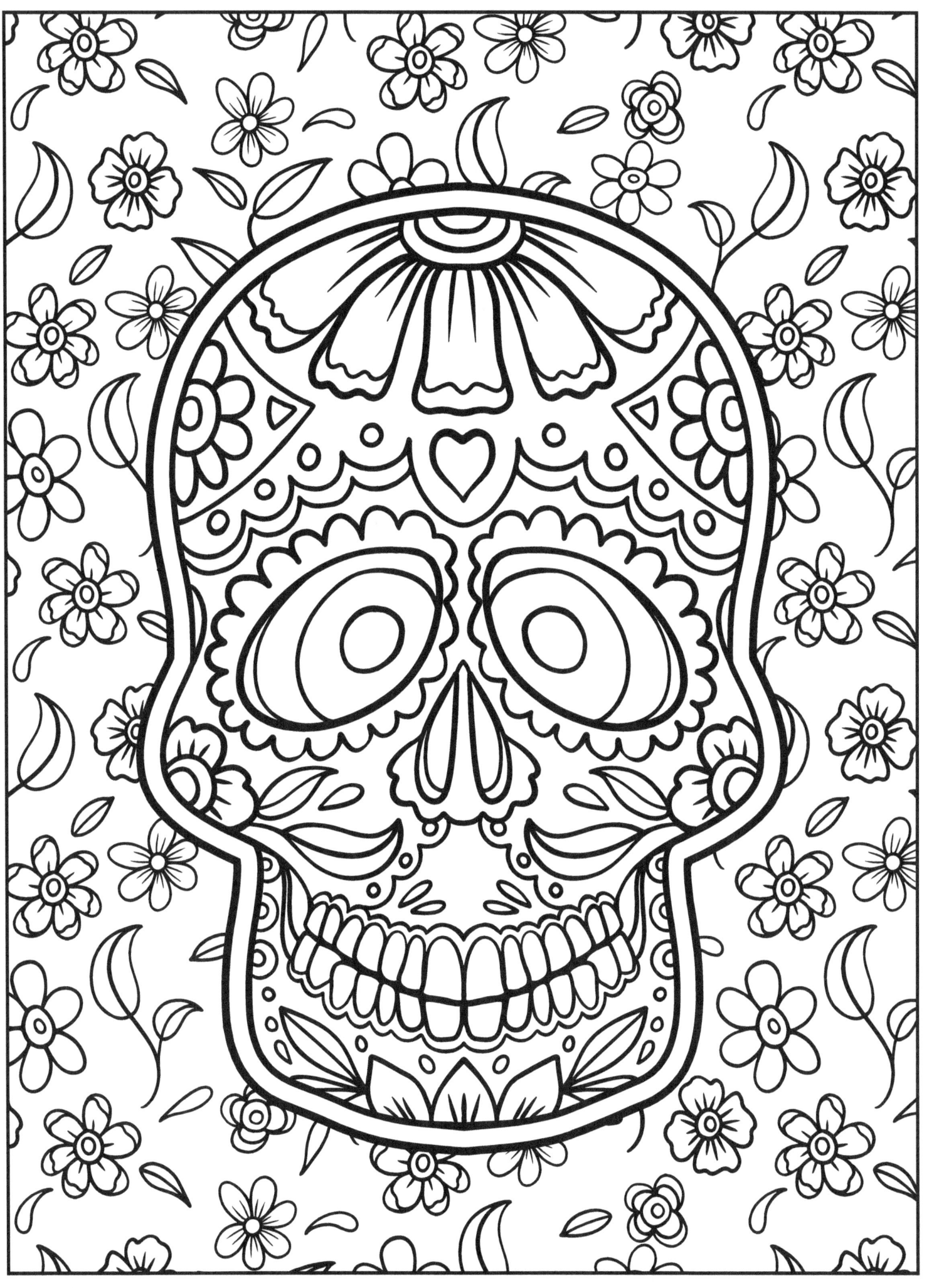

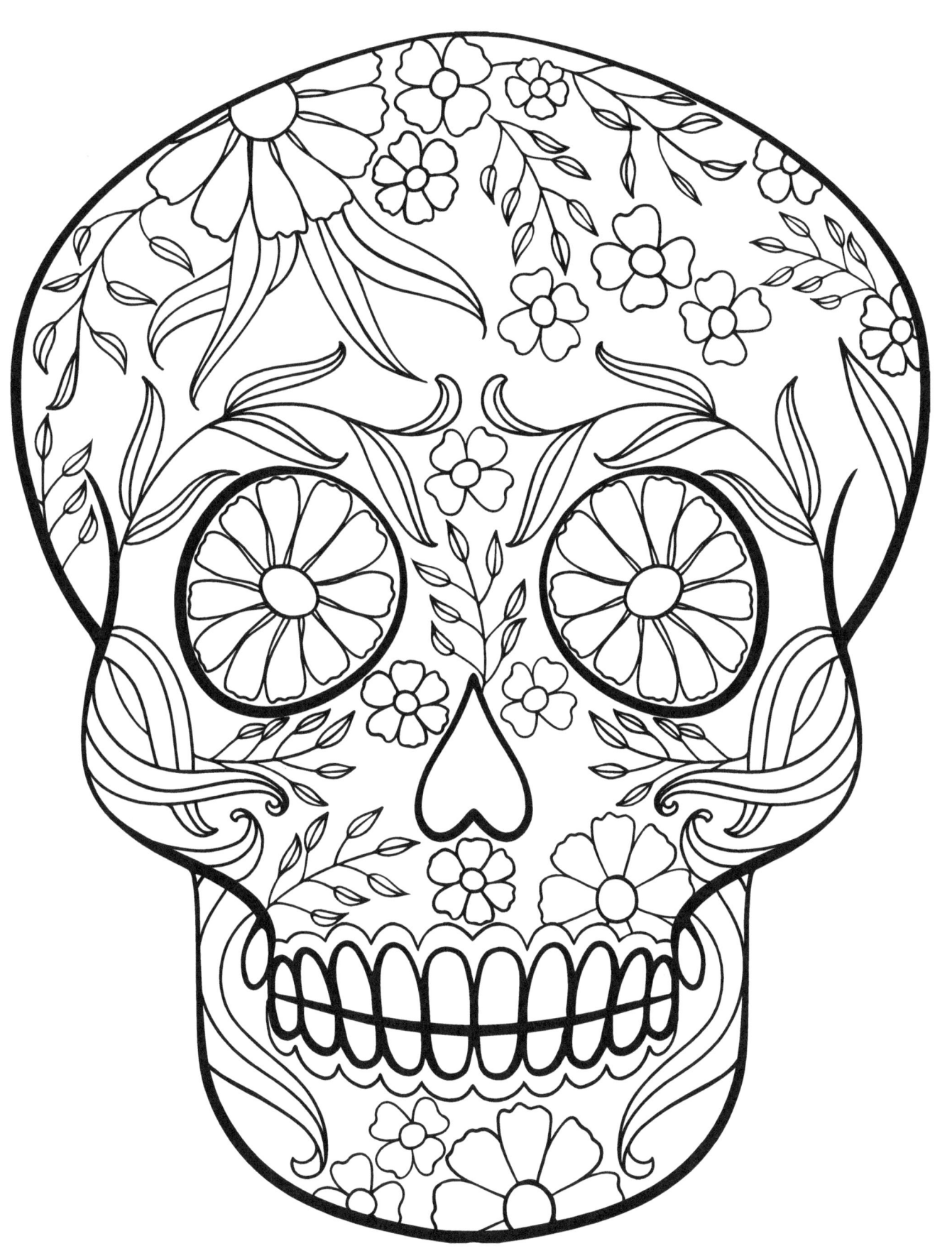

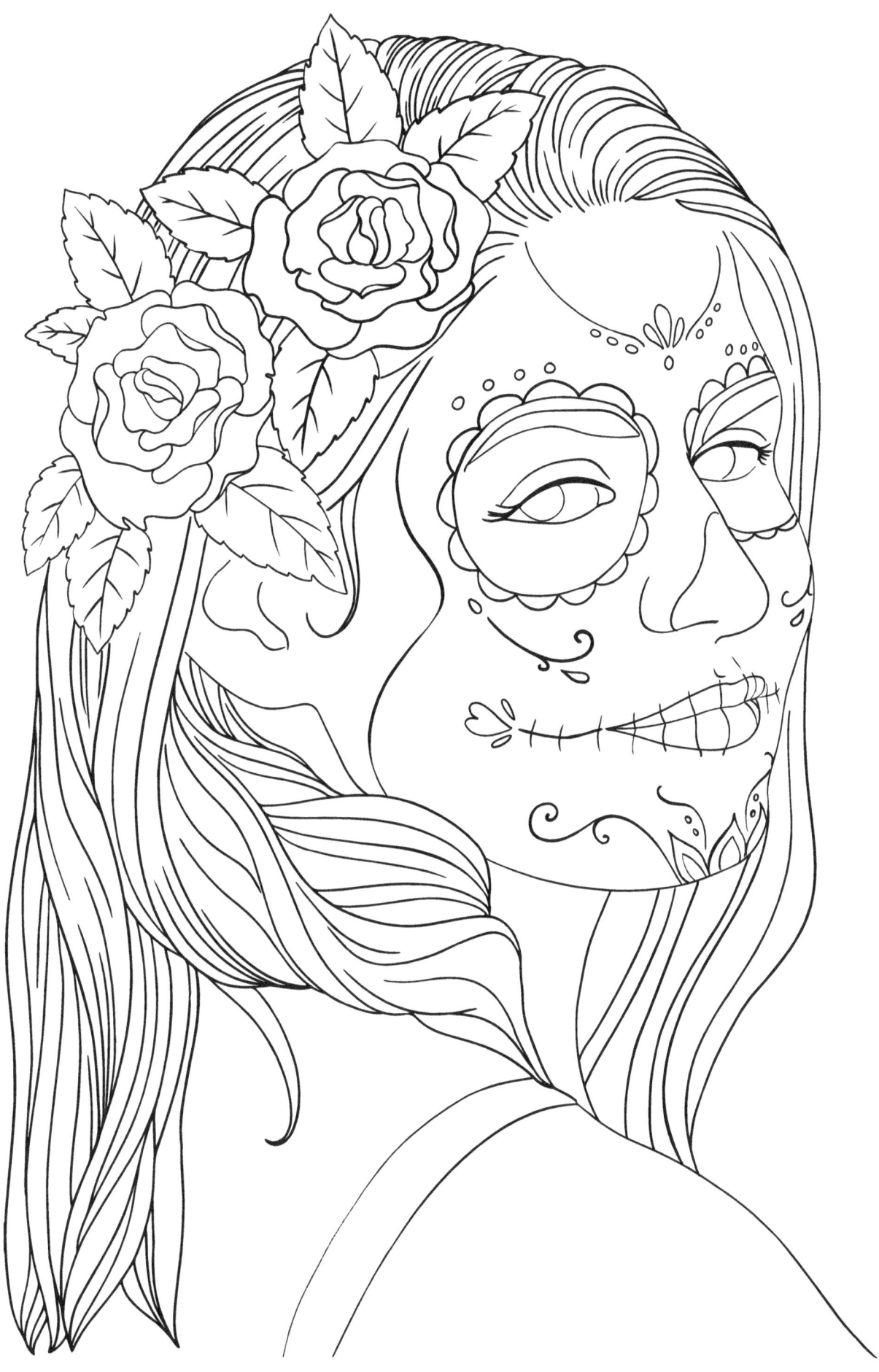

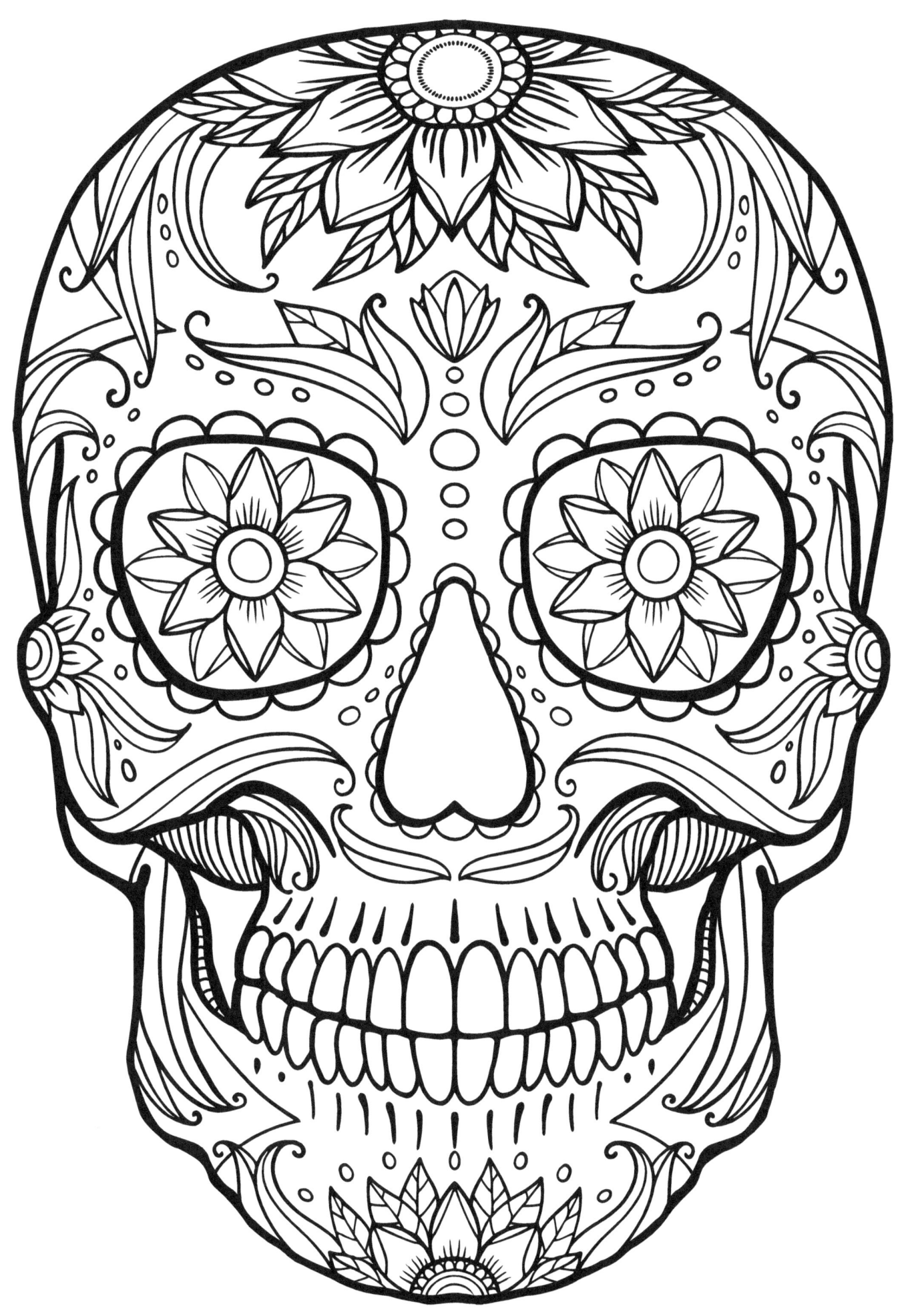

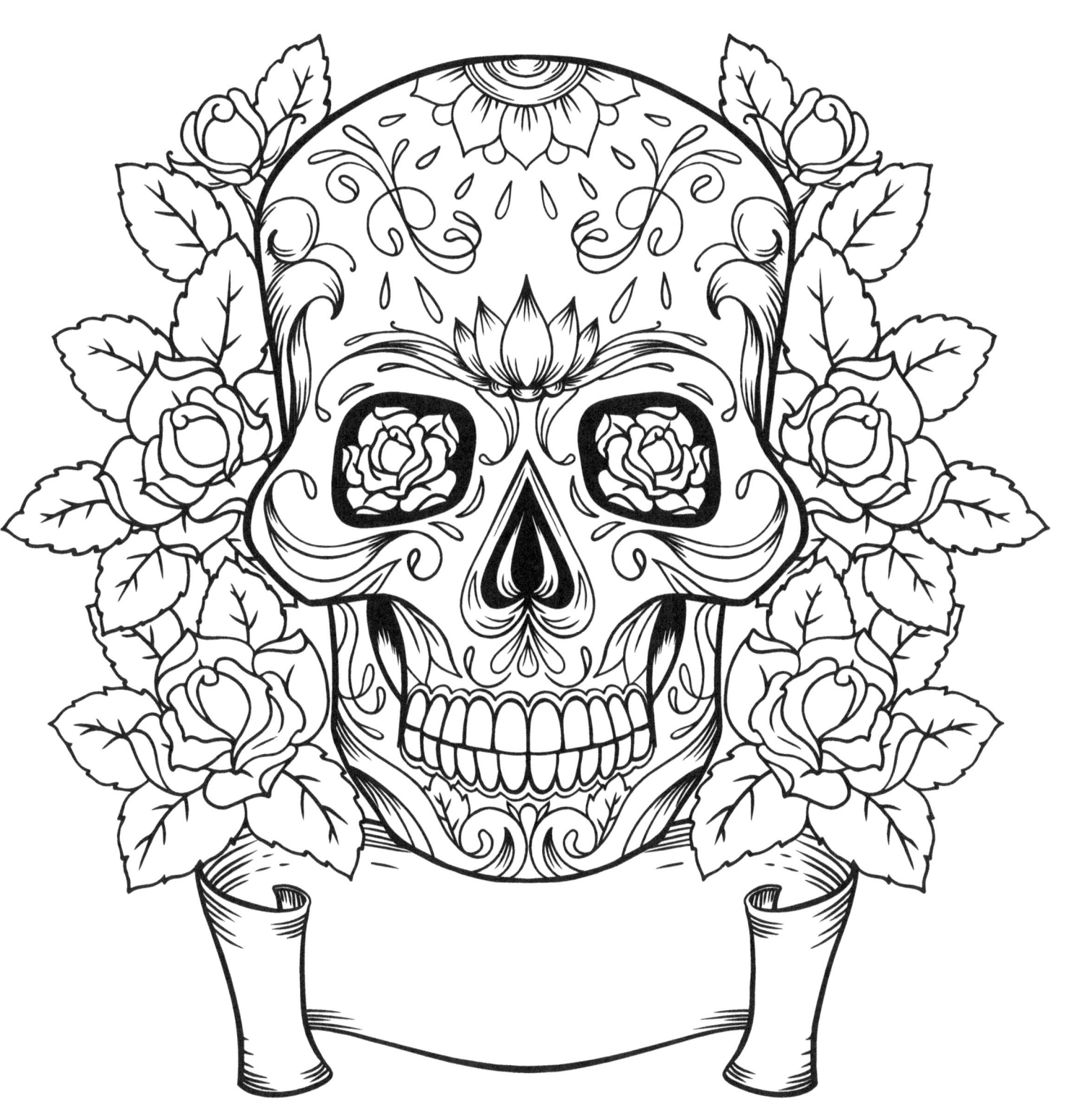

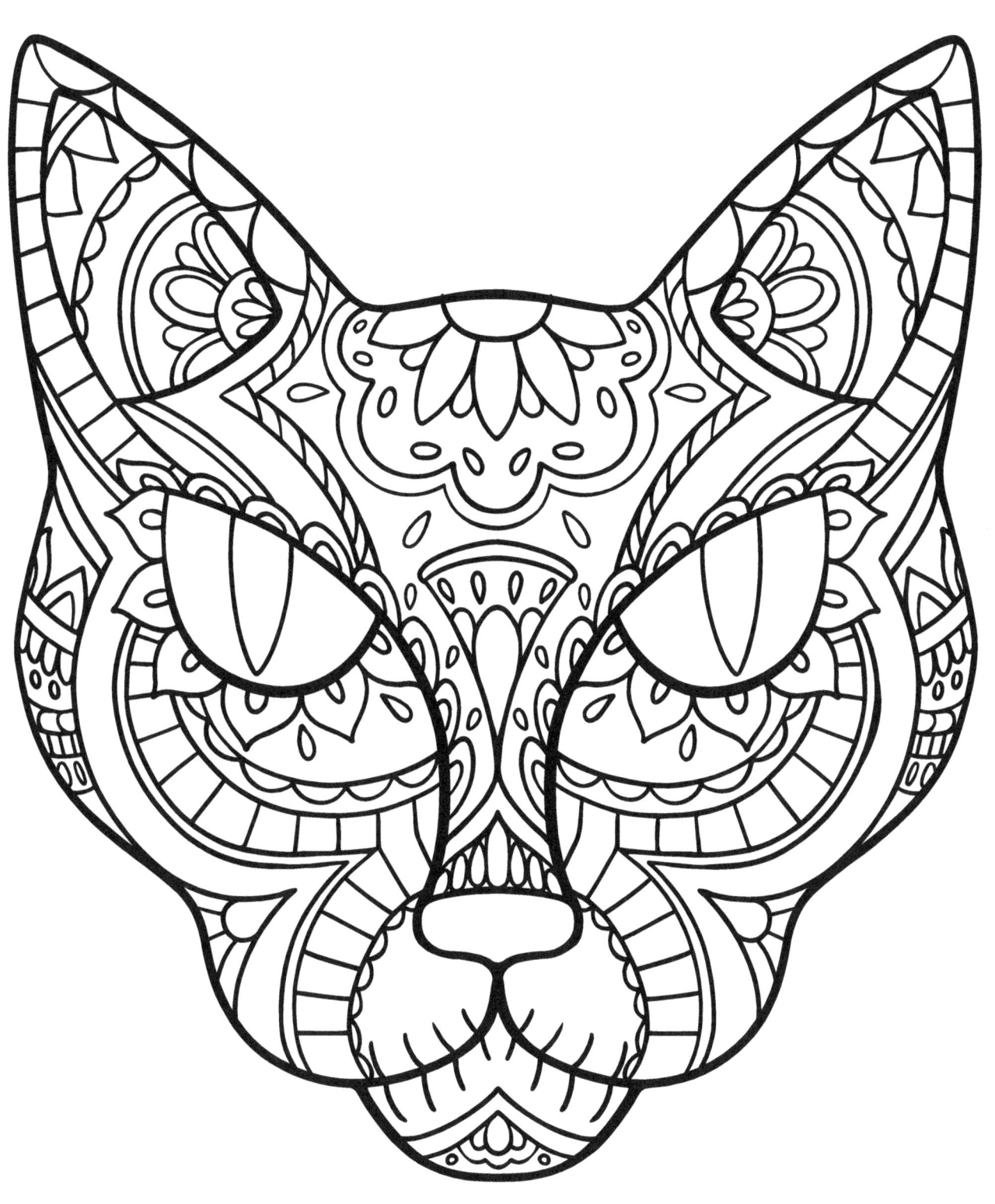

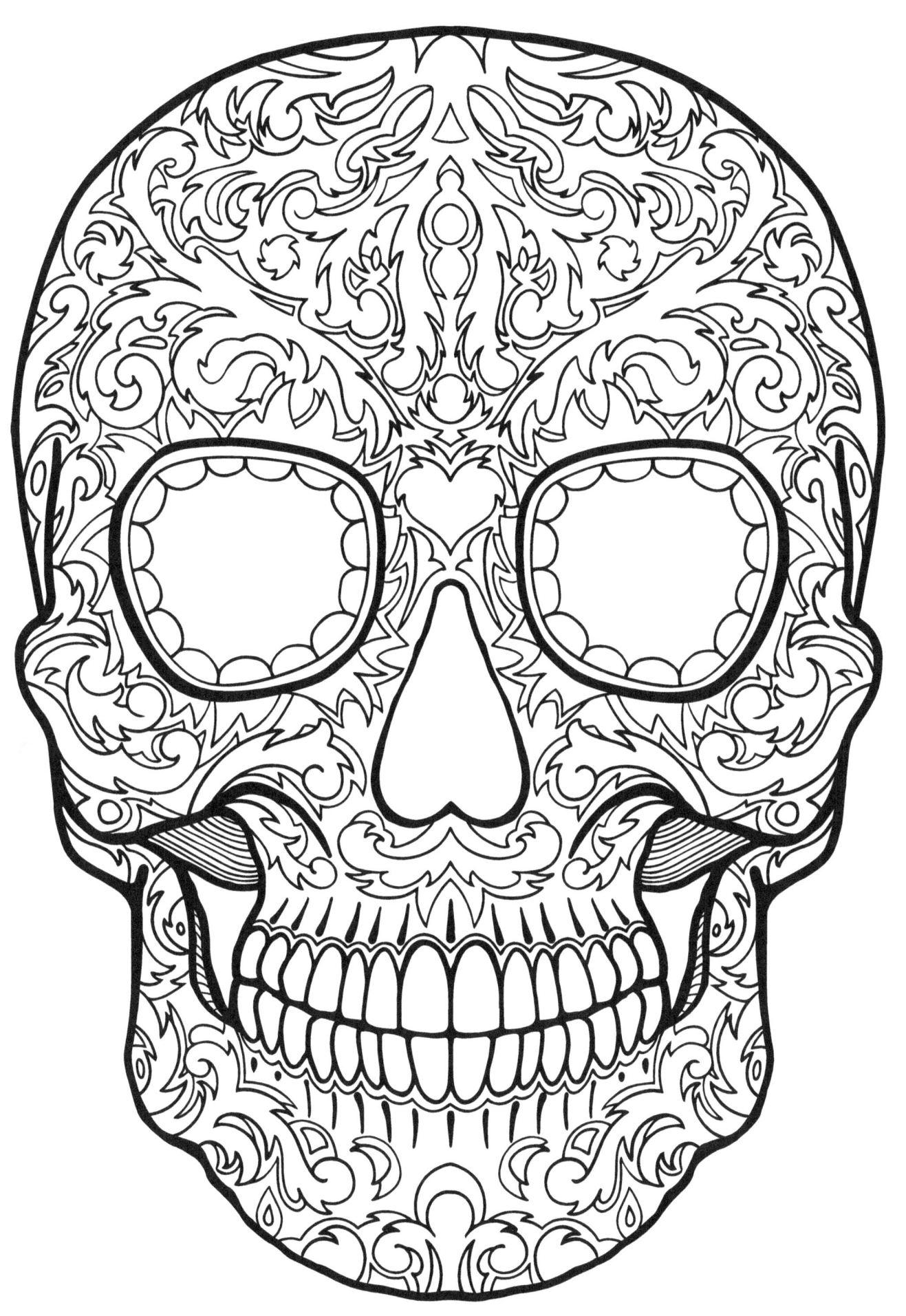

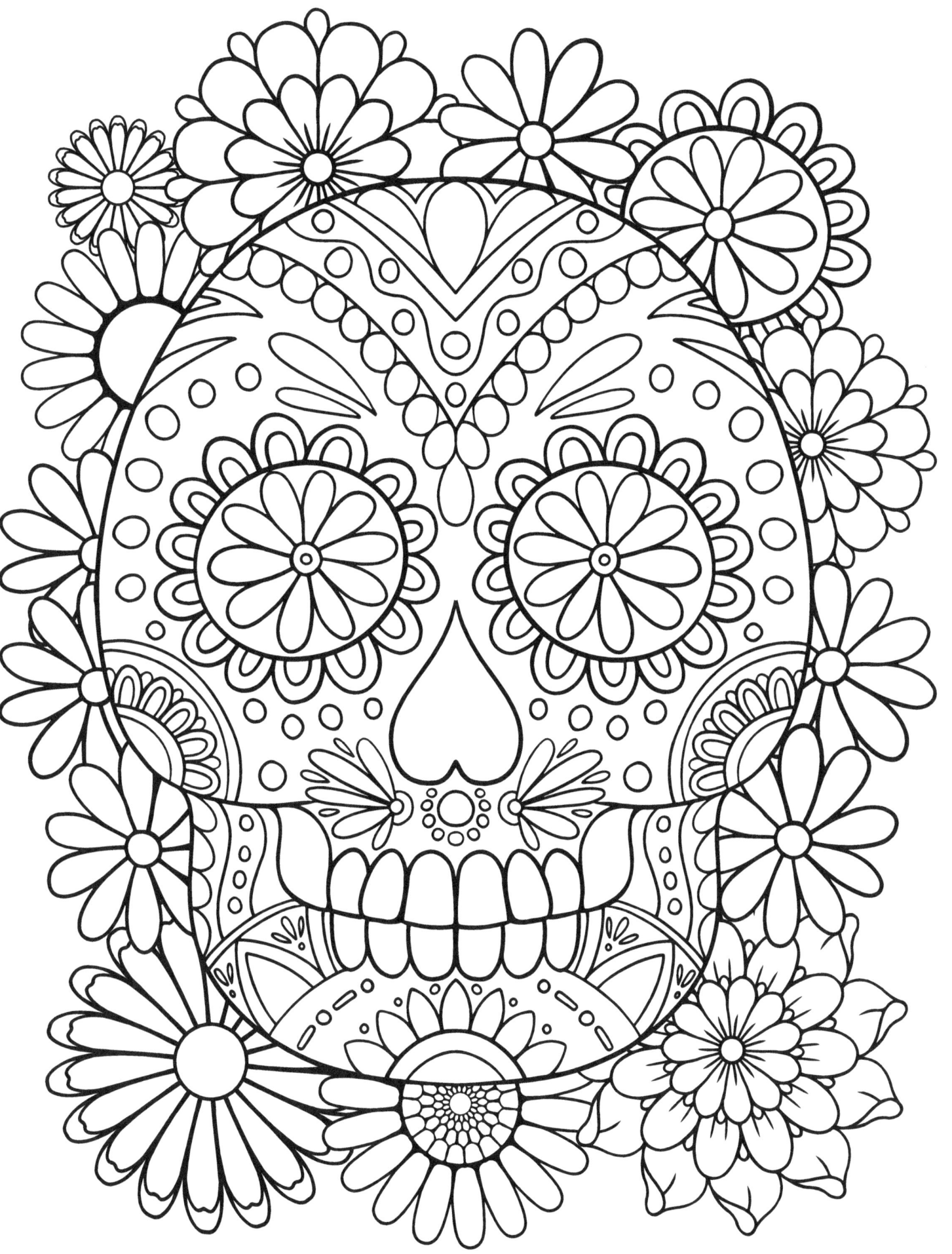

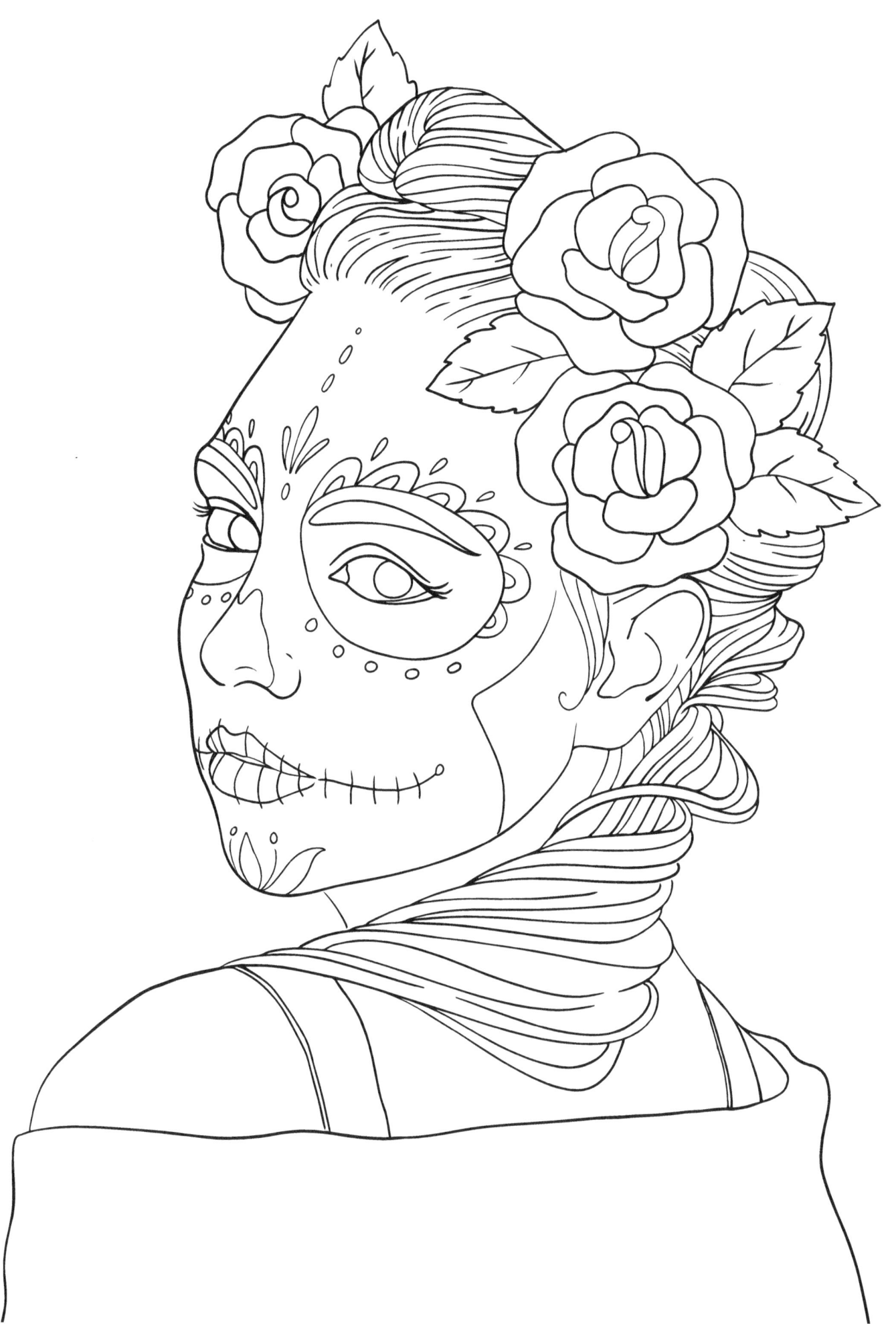

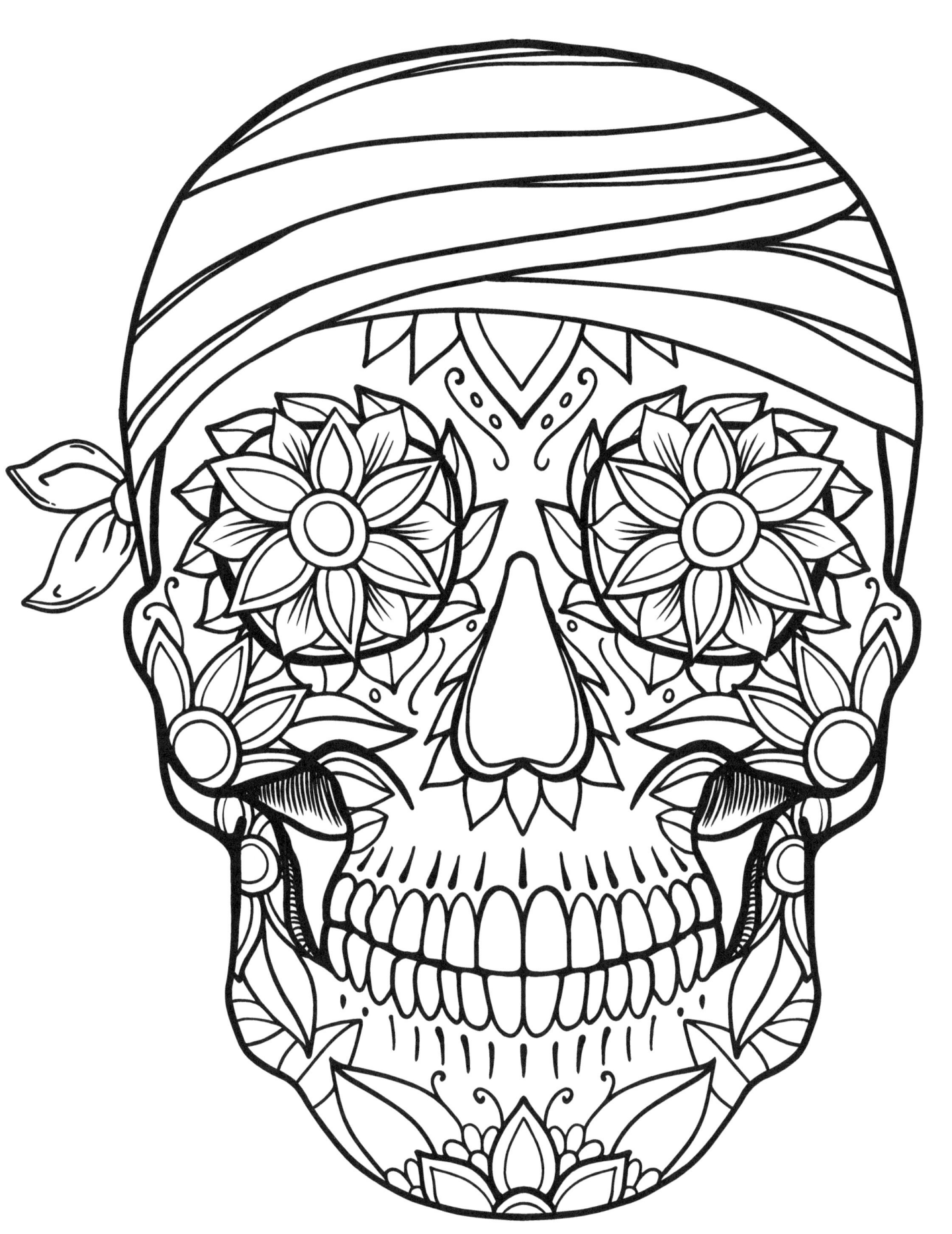

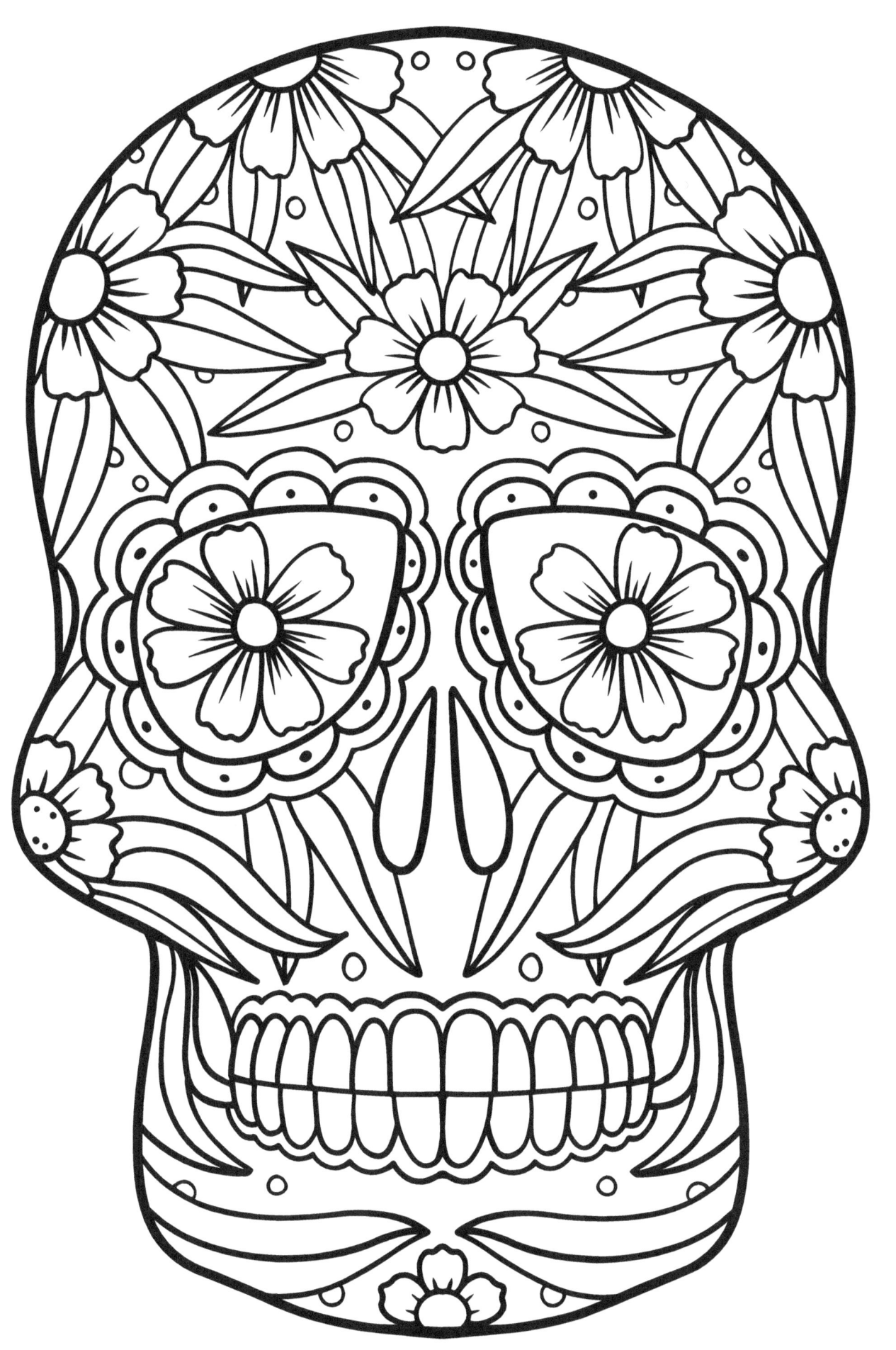

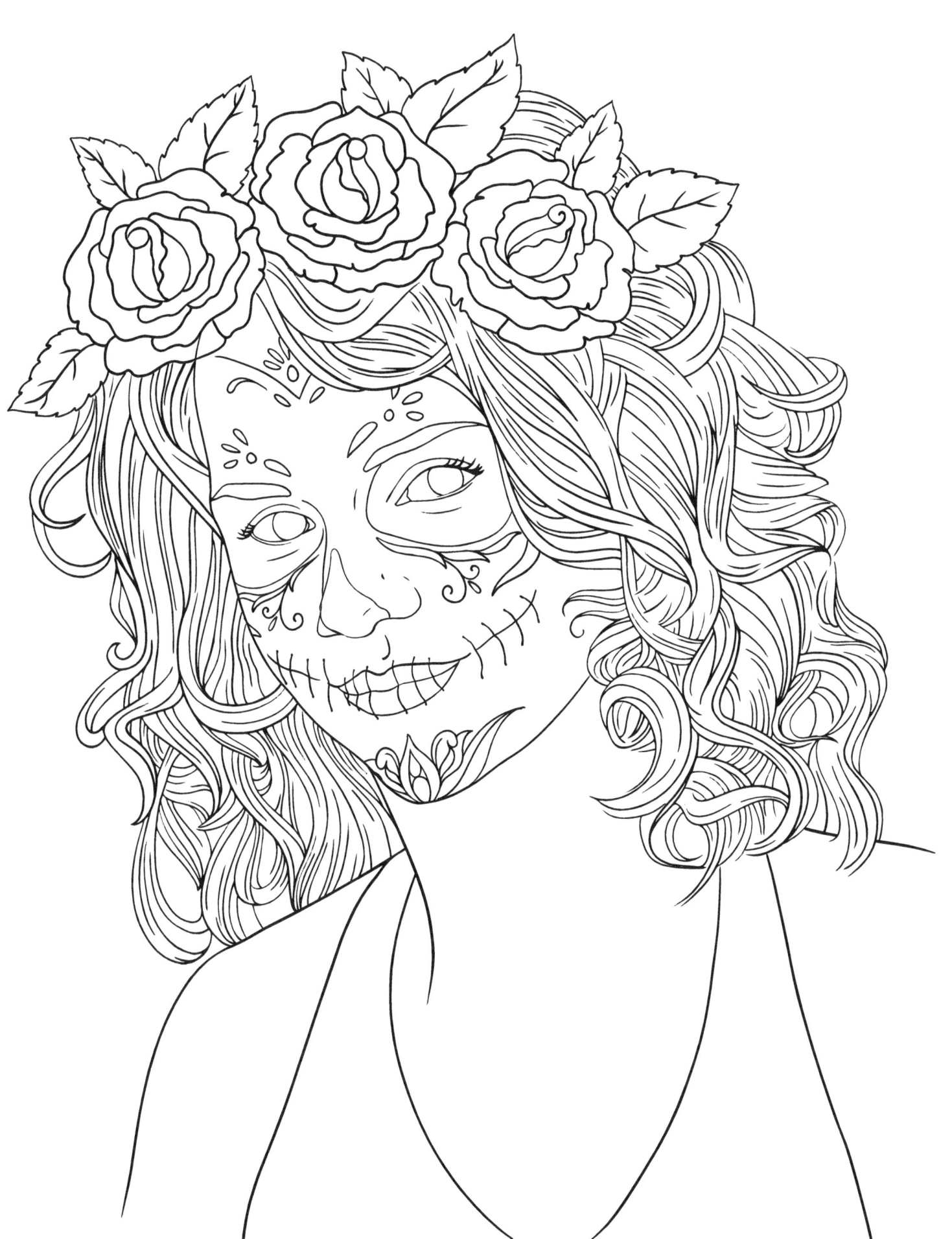

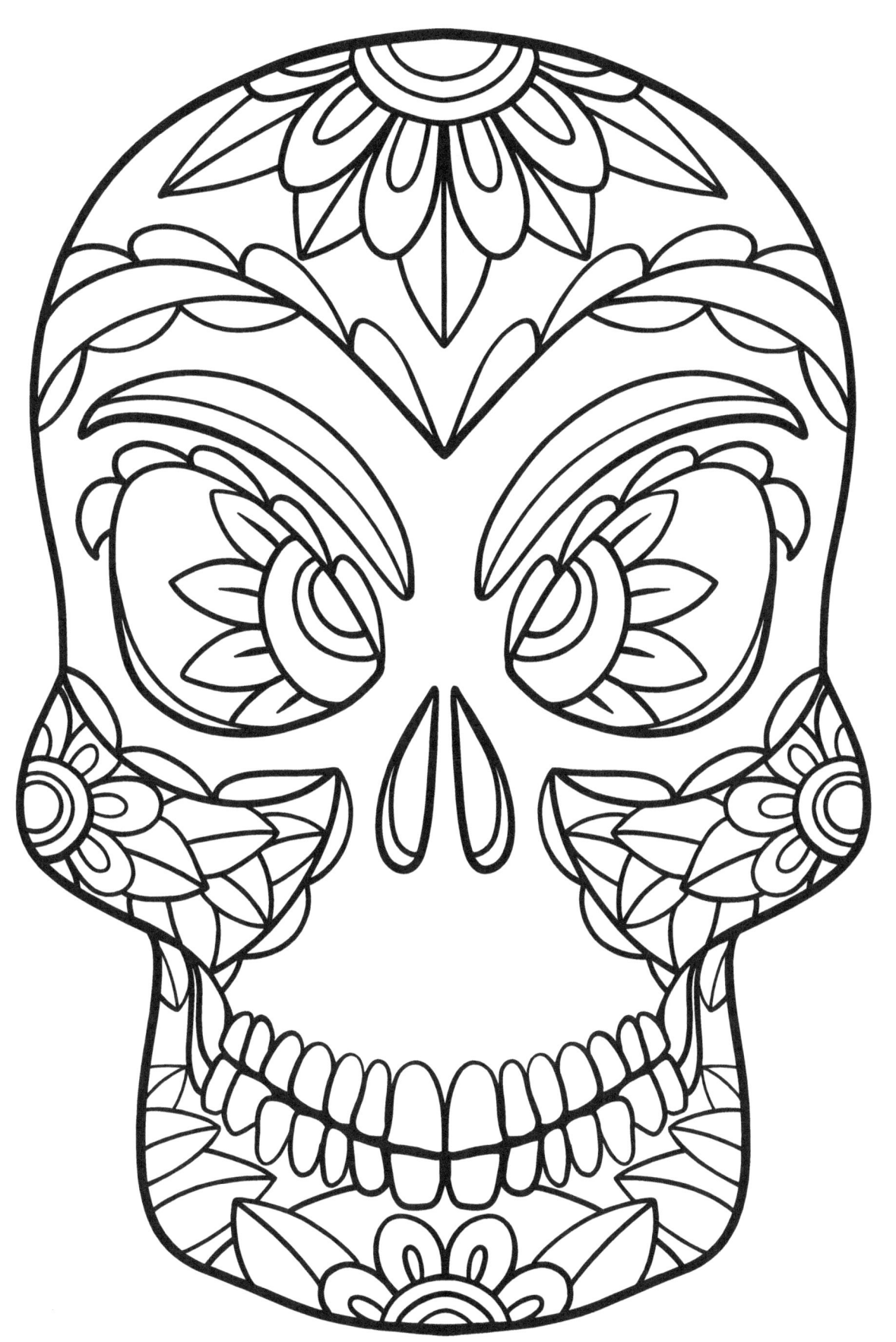